ST. ANDREWS: CITY OF CHANGE

By the same authors:
Victorian and Edwardian Fife from Rare Photographs
Victorian and Edwardian Borderland from Rare Photographs
Victorian and Edwardian Dundee and Broughty Ferry from Rare Photographs
Fife: Portrait of a County 1910-1950.

By Raymond Lamont-Brown:
The History of St Marks Church, Dewsbury
A Book of Epitaphs
Doncaster Rural District: Official Guide
Clarinda: The Intimate story of Robert Burns and Agnes Maclehose
Sir Walter Scott's Letters on Demonology and Witchcraft
A Book of Superstitions
A Book of Proverbs
A Book of Witchcraft
Robert Burns's Commonplace Book, 1783-85
Phantoms of the Sea
Charles Kirkpatrick Sharpe's Witchcraft in Scotland
General Trade in Berwick-upon-Tweed
Robert Burns's Tour of the Borders
A New Book of Epitaphs
The Magic Oracles of Japan
Robert Burns's Tours of the Highlands and Stirlingshire
A Casebook of Military Mystery
Phantoms of the Theatre
Epitaph Hunting
Scottish Epitaphs
Lothian and the Southeast Borders: Walks for Motorists
East Anglian Epitaphs
Growing Up with the Highland Clans
My Fun Book of Scotland
Mysteries and Legends
Mary Queen of Scots
Drives around Edinburgh
St Andrews: A Visitors Guide
Drives around Glasgow
Mothers-in-law

ST. ANDREWS: CITY OF CHANGE

TEXT
RAYMOND LAMONT-BROWN
PHOTOGRAPHY
PETER ADAMSON

FOREWORD
BY
JOHN STEVEN WATSON
M.A., D.Litt., D.H.L., D.H., F.R.Hist.S., F.R.S.E.
Principal and Vice-Chancellor of the University of St. Andrews

ALVIE PUBLICATIONS   ST ANDREWS

ACKNOWLEDGEMENTS

The authors would like to express their gratitude and thanks to the following for their help and encouragement in the production of the book: The Principal and Vice-Chancellor of the University, Dr John Steven Watson, for kindly writing the Foreword; Professor D.A. Bullough; Mr G. Christie; Mr R. Smart; Mrs P. Borthwick; Mr C.B. Bremner; Mr E. Malcolm; Mr R. Burnett.

Further thanks are expressed individually to the undermentioned copyright holders for their kind help and permission to reproduce photographs from their collections:

The University of St Andrews: 3, 23, 24, 30, 36, 38, 51, 52, 74.

North East Fife District Council: 4.

St Andrews Preservation Trust: 5.

Mr J.N. Walker, 72.

St Andrews Citizen: 75, 76, 77, 78.

St Leonards School: 80.

A.B. Paterson: 82.

First published in 1984 by
Alvie Publications
52 Buchanan Gardens
St Andrews KY16 9LX

ISBN 0 9506200 8 4

Printed and bound in Scotland by
Spectrum Printing Company
Edinburgh and Livingston

FOREWORD

John Steven Watson, M.A., D.Litt, D.H.L., D.H., F.R.Hist.S., F.R.S.E.
Principal and Vice Chancellor of the University of St Andrews.

THE authors have chosen a title which will startle some people. An alumnus who returns or a Scot remembering happy holidays will choose to see St. Andrews as a place that never changes. It holds so many youthful memories that if you take away its enchanted changelessness you rob them of their past. Sir James Barrie may have derived the spirit of Peter Pan as well as the legendary name of the Admirable Crichton from his time as Rector here.

Of course, there have been many visible changes even in my own time here. The escarpment of the North Haugh has been lined with buildings; many old shops have given way to branch stores. Our alumni and other *revenants* are sometimes very critical of such developments but usually they manage to ignore them. Alterations, they like to say, are superficial. The spirit of the place, the streets of small buildings, remain the same. They gaze at St. Andrews as one looks into the face of an old friend. It is true there are some new lines under the eyes, some marks of experience, perhaps new anxieties, but it has still the well-remembered, the welcoming expression of that dear old fellow we have known so long.

I am inclined, as I think of this, to wonder if the book sets out to be perverse and provoking. Then I remember that it has a very long timescale. What would the Culdees feel if they were—perhaps they do—to walk these cliffs again? All that they knew has been eroded. Just as completely the calling cards of Professors' wives and the etiquette of only a generation ago have vanished along with their carriages. They are forgotten with the monks and hermits. *Où sont les neiges d'antan?*

Sentimental remarks like that, however, could be made and are made about so many places. There is a special relationship to change in St Andrews. Here we have change which arrests decay. Every year "new blood" is pumped—or injected, or forces its way—into the veins of this old place. To several hundred talented people the great age of the world begins anew. New shoes clatter up old stairs and fresh faces quiz the way ahead. Almost at once the young heads become aware of the past, saplings discover that they have roots. As a result the more often a change of company takes place, the greater our sense of the continuity of history.

There is a serious moral here. It is impossible in St. Andrews not to be aware of tradition. But that should not make anyone an enemy of change. The motto of the University exhorts it to be continuously seeking for the best. A continuous search for excellence implies a readiness to meet new conditions with creative innovation. The only consistent and unchanging tradition in St Andrews is to aim high. That, I am resolved to think, is the significance of the book's title. The camera records page by page both the successes and the failures of those who have brought a lively spirit to the cultivation of a rare inheritance.

5

2. St Andrews from above Easter Grange Farm and the Grange cottages. Such views inspired poets like Andrew Lang (1844-1912) who wrote thus in *Almae Matres,* 'St Andrews 1862, Oxford 1865', of all the longing-love that he felt about the town:

St Andrews by the Northern Sea,
A haunted town it is to me!
A little city, worn and grey,
The grey North Ocean girds it round,
And o'er the rocks and up the bay,
The long sea-rollers surge and sound.
And still the thin and biting spray
Drives down the melancholy street,
And still endure, and still decay,
Towers that the salt winds vainly beat.
Ghost-like and shadowy they stand
Dim mirrored in the wet sea-sand . . .

O, broken minster looking forth
Beyond the bay, above the town,
O, winter of the kindly North,
O, college of the scarlet gown,
And shining sands beside the sea,
Once more I watch you, and to me
It is as if I touched his hand!

And therefore art thou yet more dear,
O, little city, grey and sere,
Though shrunken from thine ancient pride
And lonely by the lonely sea,
Than these fair halls on Isis' side,
Where youth an hour came back to me! . . .

And yet, in going on to praise Oxford's trees and countryside, Lang comes back nostalgically to:

. . . The drifting surf, the wintry year,
The college of the scarlet gown,
St Andrews by the Northern Sea
That is a haunted town to me!

1. The cathedral from Deanscourt.

7

3. The Fishers' Quarter, North St, c.1844, a calotype photograph taken by David Octavius Hill (1802-70) and Robert Adamson (1821-48).

4. St Andrews harbour in the late 19th century.

5. Sandy 'Sandshoe' Chisholm, St Andrews last surviving lifeboatman. He was in the lifeboat crew which rescued the survivors of the *Princess Wilhelmina*, 1912.

ST ANDREWS: CITY OF CHANGE

The old order changeth, yielding place to new,
And God fulfils Himself in many ways,
Lest one good custom should corrupt the world.
ALFRED, LORD TENNYSON (1809-92)
'The Passing of Arthur':
The Idylls of the King

ST ANDREWS is an enclave within Fife, a haven from man's industrial toils in the coalfields of the west of the county; an ancient city set on a wedge of land by the sea within an ocean of farmland. The environment is so explicitly individual that visitors are aware of the atmospheric change on entering and leaving the town.

St Andrews, as we know it in its location today, began as a Pictish settlement, although there was probably a sizeable population living hereabouts from mid-Neolithic times, sometime before 1900 BC. A romantic-sounding people, the Picts—their name comes from *Picti,* the Latin participle for 'painted,'—were the *dramatis personae* of Dark Age Scotland. Small, dark folk, who covered themselves with tattoos of rank or devotion to long-forgotten gods, the Picts fished the waters of St Andrews Bay, hunted the forests of the East Neuk and tilled the ridges above and around the modern town. They fished to stay alive, and 3500 years later there had developed a community which was still plying the same craft.

One of the first well-defined *quartiers* of St Andrews was that of the fishing families who dwelt at the Lady Head. In medieval times the Fisher Cross stood near the crossroads made by North Street and the two Castle Streets. Abutting the cathedral wall, the fishermen had their own school and meeting places. Women would sit at their doors 'reddin' and baiting the lines. The Mussel Scalps, gathered on the Eden, belonged to the town and those were an important source of bait. In the 1850's St Andrews had around an hundred fishermen and some 14 boats. In 1911 the correspondent of the *Fife News Almanac* had this to say: 'The fishing industry at St Andrews has never been very prosperous owing to the dangerous nature of the Bay, and the steam trawler having made the lot of the old-fashioned fishermen even harder. The fishing population at St Andrews . . . is slowly passing away.'

During the winter, haddock were fairly plentiful in St Andrews Bay, and in February and March good catches of plaice were to be had. It was not uncommon, of course, for St Andrews boats to range some 80 miles into the North Sea, with a favourite fishing area called 'The Long Forties' (ie, at a depth of forty fathoms). The fish was sold at St Andrews harbour.

St Andrews harbour is tidal and stands at the estuary of the Kinness Burn, and these days sees more pleasure craft than fishing boats. Sea trips from the harbour were very popular before World War I. The pier was once constructed of wood and extended further out to sea; this pier was badly damaged in the great storm of 1655, and in 1656 the timber, slates and stone from the castle were sold to defray repairs. In time castle stone was used to re-build the pier. During the Senzie Fair of the Middle Ages it is recorded that hundreds of vessels tied up in St Andrews harbour, but the opening of the railway made the harbour decline—as did the steam trawling which killed off the local herring trade. Yet, within living memory, schooners and sloops crowded the harbour to trade in coal and wood. In 1897 responsibility for the harbour was passed from the Town Council to the Harbour Trust. Again during 1926-47 the pier was in poor repair, but various local public bodies gave assistance towards the cost of repairs. Of course, the port of St Andrews in medieval times was a few miles away at the mouth of the Motray Burn near modern Guardbridge.

The pier is the setting for the traditional 'walk' by students in their red gowns on Sunday morning after chapel. The tradition began in 1911 when the then Rector, Archibald Philip Primrose, 5th Earl of Roseberry (1847-1929, Home Rule Liberal Prime Minister 1894-95) arrived in his yacht during a fine September afternoon for the university's quincentenary celebrations. The students met the Rector—for the first time in history at the end of the pier—and escorted him to his waiting carriage at the top of Kirk Hill. Incidentally students have worn scarlet since the Reformation, and it is thought that the custom may have been introduced in the reign of James VI. The black gowns of the theological students of St Mary's College date from 1856, and are distinctive with their violet cross on the left facing. The conventions of wearing gowns have changed little since the 19th century. *Bejants* (cf. *béjaune* a fledgling in French falconry) wear the gown full on; *Semis* wear them lower over the shoulder; *Tertians* wear them drooped over one shoulder; and, *Magistrands* wear them trailing over both shoulders.

6. Panoramic views have long been popular from St Rule's Tower.

7. (facing page) The east end of the cathedral seen through the vestibule of the old chapter-house.

The fisherfolk were a colourful and individual breed, easily distinguishable from their fellow-St Andreans by their blue jerseys and peak caps. Superstitious by nature, they sported many a nickname to differentiate those of the same surname. Families like the Gourlays, the Wilsons, the Chisholms and the Waters had fished for generations, and many of them were classed as 'characters'. One such was Mrs Henry Clark, universally known as 'Joan', who died 4th September 1927, aged 75. She was working up to ten months before her death, and she always wore the traditional Scots fishwife's garb of white stockings, black elastic-sided boots, striped skirt over voluminous petticoats, tight bodice, red shawl and fisher apron. Joan earned her living selling fish from her barrow to the St Andrews housewives; fish she had bought from the East Neuk cadgers. 'Joan's House', a small pantiled house with a curved forestair, is still to be seen at 11 South Castle Street and is perhaps the most picturesque relic of the old fishing quarter. As the fishing trade declined, many of the redundant fishermen became golf caddies.

While archaeology occasionally turns up a relic of Dark Age St Andrews, it is to the ecclesiastics that we have to look for historical material about the first developments hereabouts. It is said that the first precise date alluding to St Andrews is 747 AD, the date of the death of Abbot Tuathala of *Cendrigmonaid.* This was recorded by the usually reliable Irish analyst Tigernach some four centuries after the event, but it gives a note of the early names of the settlement that was to bloom as St Andrews. *Cendrigmonaid* is Gaelic for 'the headland of the king's hill'. To this place, a 12th century chronicle says, came the monk Regulus from Constantinople with the relics of St Andrew the Apostle and Martyr. Of Bethsaida in Galilee, Andrew was the first Apostle called by Christ, and was the brother of Simon Peter. He was martyred by the Romans who scourged him and bound him to a cross (not nailed, that his death might be more lingering) where he hung for two days before death. In a dream, the chroniclers said, Regulus was warned that Andrew's bones were to be desecrated by the Emperor Constantine, so he voyaged 'to the uttermost ends of the earth' arriving at the Pictish settlement at 'the summit of the king's hill that is Rigmund', within Muckross 'the headland of the swine'. So legend linked *Cendrigmonaid* with St Andrews and his cross decussate, and so the holy myth created the spiritual foundation of modern St Andrews. At the Kate Kennedy pageant St Andrew leads the procession bearing his cross of martyrdom, the Saltire of the Scottish Flag.

The 'headland of the king's hill' was to be the focal point of all the events that gave St Andrews its prominence and that occurrence which caused the once proud city to fall into decline. We do not know exactly when Christianity first came to St Andrews, yet it appears that the first named professional Christian to be associated with St Andrews was the Irishman, St Cainnech, who is reported as having a hermitage at *Cendrigmonaid,* by-named Kilrymont. Cainnech was a contemporary and friend of the Irish founder of the monastery at Iona, the missionary, St Columba. So, although a Roman Christian, soldier or merchant may have tramped the coast of the East Neuk and spoken of Christ, the religion as a going concern was established here around 550 AD.

Christianity was not properly developed in St Andrews until around 732-747 when the Pictish High King, Angus I, brought relics of St Andrew from the Anglo-Saxon cathedral at Hexham, Northumberland, which St Wilfred of York had built around 674. To Hexham, Bishop Acca had brought relics of the saint to which the cathedral was dedicated, and it was these relics which had been 'acquired' by Angus I when the bishop fell into disfavour in 732.

So by now we seemingly have stories concerning two lots of relics: those brought by one Regulus, and those acquired by Angus. Which story is correct is a matter of which myth is to be accepted, rather than any historical proof. It is likely that we shall never know, as they could be the same bones confusingly described by some inky-fingered cleric. How relics of St Andrew came to St Andrews . . . and whether or not they were animal bones, or bones of someone else, or pieces of the Apostle's garments sold to the clergy by some con-man . . . remains a historical mystery. But, suffice it to say, bones or no bones, by 761 a Christian community was established at Muckross headland sanctified by the name of the Apostle.

St Andrews has seen three aspects of organised Christianity. Up to around 1100 there was a period of uncertain religious development, with known bishops from the tenth century. The Medieval Chruch (ie, made 'Roman Catholic' by the coming of Protestantism) ruled from *circa* 1100 to 1560 and, after 1560, came the Reformed Church which gave birth to the 'Church of Scotland'. After 1560, of course there was still an episcopal presence in St Andrews in the body of Archbishop Patrick Adamson who held office until 1592. Today three ruins spell out in stone the changes in Christian worship in St Andrews: the Collegiate Church and Chapel Royal of the Blessed Mary on the Rock; St Rule's Tower and Chapel; and the cathedral.

The ruin of the Church of St Mary on the Rock is set on the Kirk Hill to the north of the cathedral

8. One hundred and eighty degree view of the old cathedral burial ground, the domestic range of the priory buildings, and the medieval street plan from St Rule's Tower. Note the coffins lying open in the floor of the 14th century chapter-house.

precinct. It is believed that here there was a still older Culdee Church (from *céli dé*, 'companions of God', a class of reformed clergy who are recorded as being in existence in the first half of the ninth century), but its history has been completely erased. The foundations seen today were excavated in 1860 when the ground was being levelled thereabouts for a gun emplacement; sculptured stones found during the excavations are to be seen in the cathedral museum. It is an old tradition that this church was first built on a rock beyond the end of the pier, and that as the sea encroached the site was abandoned. It is, of course, a matter of conjecture that the church's title of 'on the Rock' refers to the old siting. Around this church on Kirk Hill there would be some kind of 'monastery' with dwellings for the priesthood. The Culdees, having a devotion too, to St Anthony the first hermit, survived as a separate ascetic group distinct from the priests of the cathedral and priory, until about 1300.

St Regulus's, or St Rule's, Tower and Church, have caused decades of historians serious questions of analysis. It was certainly the predecessor of the cathedral and is Romanesque in style, an architectural form which was present in European art into the twelfth century. The church has seen many architectural changes, as witnessed in the stonework, and probably dates in its inception to *circa* 1127-44. Of 108ft in height, and set on a base 20ft square, the tower had a stairway set in its present form *circa* 1779 and forms a favourite bird's-eye view of the town for both visitor and photographer. Below are placed generations of citizens who lie in their narrow cells; behind the curtain wall of the cathedral burial ground lies the more modern Eastern Cemetery where the clerics once had a Holy Well. Between the Holy Well and the cathedral ruins were sited the priory granary and workshops in medieval times. At these workshops were probably fired the tiles, still to be seen in the cathedral nave.

The bitter changes of fierce extremes within religious philosophy are seen no better than at the cathedral. There, change and decay are all around. The establishment of the cathedral and priory of St Andrews was an important development in the history of the town, and its presence was to give the royal burgh international fame and national primacy. The cathedral, the largest building ever erected in medieval Scotland, was to have a dual function. It was the cathedral church of the diocese of St Andrews, and the church of the Augustinian Order of Canons Regular who were resident at the priory. The priory itself formed the range of domestic buildings to the south side of the cathedral church and were in the control of a prior. Today, two clergymen have St Andrews in their titles; The Episcopal Bishop of St Andrews, Dunkeld and Dunblane, and, the Roman Catholic Archbishop of St Andrews and Edinburgh. The very last pre-Reformation Archbishop of St Andrews was John Hamilton (1512-71), who was executed in full pontifical vestments at Stirling for his alleged complicity in the murder of Mary Queen of Scots's second husband, Henry Darnley. A Benedictine monk, Hamilton had engendered much hatred by ordering the execution by burning of Walter Myln, the octogenarian Lutheran priest, in 1558 (Myln is especially commemmorated by a cross on the cobbles outside Deanscourt).

The cathedral church was structurally founded 1160-61 by Arnold, Abbot of Kelso, with the active promotion of King Malcolm IV of the House of Dunkeld. The great cathedral represents active architectural work from the 12th to the 16th centuries and was consecrated by Bishop William Lamberton (1265-1328) in the presence of King Robert I, the Bruce, on 5th July 1318. The stone for its fabrication came from the nearby quarries of Strathkinness and Kinkell. In 1472 the diocese was erected into the dignatory of an archiepiscopal and metropolitan see. In 1487 Pope Innocent VIII made the cathedral into the seat of the Primate of All Scotland. The first prelate to become archbishop was Patrick Graham, a former Bishop of Brechin, who had secured a bull of erection from Sixtus IV; thereafter the cathedral became the main seat of jurisdiction of the *Ecclesia Scoticana*.

The height of the cathedral grandure was around 1440-1559. As the relic shell of this great church—famous all over Europe for the intensity of its apostolate—is viewed today, it is difficult to visualise the rich hangings, the tessellated pavements, the embroidered vestments, the stained glass, the paintings, the chalices, the pattens and the alms-dishes all of chased gold (indeed the cathedral contained an enormous part of the medieval artistic heritage of Scotland). The focal point of worship was the high altar flanked by the statues of St Andrew and the Virgin Mary. Brightly coloured and encrusted with *ex voto* offerings, these statues were probably gifted by the family of the Earls of Douglas. Behind the high altar and secured by locked doors to right and left of the altar screen, was the Chapel of Relics. Only privileged people would be allowed inside to view such of the cathedral treasures as the crystal cross from the field of Bannockburn, 1314, and the Reliquary of St Margaret. There day and night, the relics of St Andrew— 'the legend' talks of an arm-bone, three fingers of the right hand, a tooth and one of the Apostle's kneecaps—were watched and reverently cared-for by the clergy. To St Andrews came pilgrims from all over Europe to pray at the Shrine of St Andrew, and kings and princes gave lavishly for the decoration of

9. The sanctuary and east end of the cathedral seen through the west door down the nave; the cathedral well is set before the transeptal crossing.

15

10.   A winter view of the east gable of the cathedral and St Rule's Tower from Gregory Place.

the ossuary casket and the shrine itself. When Edward I visited St Andrews in 1304-05 with his second wife, Margaret of France, he gave a gift of jewels for the reliquary.

The cathedral is in the shape of a Latin cross and has an extreme length of 391 ft, second only to Norwich. The east end, the south transept and the remaining nave wall are of Romanesque style, while the great west gable is 13th century. When complete the cathedral was of twelve nave bays, a crossing with central tower, north and south transepts, and a choir of six bays. In the centre of the nave is a well, which probably had a fine ornamental well-head and maybe a canopy. This well probably originally supplied water for the construction, and would be used latterly to draw water for liturgical ceremonies, vessel washing and floor scouring. Set within the cathedral were 31 altars including one to St Thomas of Canterbury (Archbishop Becket, 1118-70) whose feast of 29th December was especially celebrated. The cathedral was dedicated to the Blessed Virgin Mary and to St Andrew. Succeeding bishops played a part in the advancing of the work, but the day to day supervision of construction was in the say of the sacrist as 'master of the fabric', working with a master mason.

The cathedral itself saw many important and political occasions. Here before the high altar King James V was married to Marie de Guise-Lorraine in 1538, and, within the cathedral, the martyrs, Patrick Hamilton, George Wishart and Walter Myln, were tried and condemned. The presence of Marie de Guise-Lorraine in St Andrews gave the chroniclers of the time a chance to record changes that had taken place in the town, now long enobled as a city because of its completed cathedral and archiepiscopate. Landing at Balcomie Beach—some ten miles away down the coast—on Trinity Sunday 1538, Marie's cavalcade paused at the New Abbey Gate and here the new queen was to witness a welcoming pageant in Latin devised by James V's old friend, Sir David Lindsay of the Mount (1486-1555), the Lord Lyon of Scotland. Then her party passed through the Pends gate, the 14th century gateway into the cathedral precinct, and thence to her lodgings. Marie was to stay at the recently-completed guest house (the priory had had a guest house for pilgrims and strangers from the 13th century) known as the *Hospitium Novum,* or New Inns. On the day after the ceremony James and Marie did a tour of the city with the provost and burgesses, and it is recorded that they stayed in St Andrews for forty days.

During the wicked days of 11th-14th June, 1559 the fanatical Scottish Reformer, John Knox (1512-72), preached in Holy Trinity Church on the biblical ejection of the buyers and sellers from the temple (*John* 2, 15). With him at the time were the armed followers of Lord James, the Earl of Argyll, Lord Ruthven, John Erskine of Dun and Wishart of Pittarrow, all rapacious 'Lords of the Congregation' who planned the attack on the cathedral. Knox would have us believe that, on hearing his words, 'the provost and baillies, as the commons for the most part within the town, did agree to remove all monuments of idolatry, which they also did with expedition.' In reality it was more likely to have been an organised and well-stagemanaged sacking by the followers of Knox to destroy the altars, images of saints, furniture, vestments, liturgical books and all the imagery and symbols of popery and Marism and, in the name of the people, to pocket all saleable booty, to which Knox's sermon was just window-dressing.

There is no evidence to show that the cathedral itself was burned or destroyed at the Reformation, but the tombs certainly were. The cathedral contained dozens of vividly coloured and richly ornamented tombs, and particular targets for vandalism were the altar-tombs of the prelates, which the Reformers reasoned correctly would contain ornate croziers, rings and personal Mass vessels of precious metal. The whole act of destruction, of course led to the vanishing of the craft beauties of medieval Scotland and hardly any gold and silver plate of the period survives.

What the actions of the priests of the cathedral were, when they knew that the mob was approaching the church with evil intent, has long been a matter of supposition. There are no records of resistance, and indeed what could the priests have done faced with an armed and hostile mob? As the grubby Calvinist fingers ripped at the gold plate on St Andrew's Shrine, the priests and novices could only pray for deliverance . . . *Pater noster qui es in caelis, sanctificetur nomen tuum* . . . Certainly as the storm of the Reformation was about to gather much of the cathedral plate may have been carried off for safe-keeping, and maybe the relics of St Andrew were moved too, to be secreted, some said, within the walls of the priory itself, where some future miracle will reveal their exact position.

After the roof lead had been purloined, the decay of the cathedral building would be made more rapid. Undoubtedly the cathedral was used as a quarry by local masons. Indeed, in 1649 Parliament authorised the Town Council to use the stones of both cathedral and priory to fortify the town.

To the south of the cathedral are ranged the domestic and office buildings of the priory, set around a cloister. Today the 13th century vestibule (Old Chapter-house) leads into the 14th century Chapter-house and the coffins of past priors. Down the side of the Chapter-house, and linking the cloisters to the cathedral graveyard, was a passage known as a slype, which is still to be seen with its open drain. The relic warming-house and the undercroft of the frater are still to be seen too, with the rere-dorter (*necessarium*) to the south of the site. To the southeast is the *Hospitium Vetus,* the Prior's House, whose ground floor now houses the cathedral museum. The cloister was used for teaching and perambulation while meditating, and an important claustral chamber was the *scriptorium,* where the vellum (skin of calves) and parchment (skin of sheep) documents were prepared; herein too, was conducted the munimentory business, the worn-out service books were repaired, as well as the daily chronicles of the priory written.

All round the priory and the 30 acre domestic site is the 20ft high Precinct Wall, inserted into which were once 16 towers of which 12 remain, and the great gateways of the Pends, the Teinds Yett, and the Mill Port. The panels in the towers attest to the fact that the wall was constructed and re-constructed by Prior John Hepburn (c.1460-1522) and his successor and nephew Patrick Hepburn, Bishop of Moray, one of the most immoral of the pre-Reformation prelates.

In 1826 the cathedral ruins were taken over by the Barons of the Exchequer and excavated, and in 1946 the priory was given to the then Ministry of Works (now Department of the Environment. The immediate environs to the north and east of the cathedral were extensively used as burial areas and it is known that interments took place in the cathedral nave up to 1834. The Chapter House was excavated 1904-05, and at that time too, a large quantity of coloured window-glass was found in the north transept. There is no historical record that the priory buildings were destroyed or damaged at the Reformation.

That part of the priory which probably housed the cellerage, with the sub-prior's lodging above, was used for a 19th century mansion house, and the cloisters were given over to a garden with greenhouses abutting the nave wall. The property was acquired by the Marquis of Bute in 1894. Within the cloisters was held the Senzie Fair in medieval times (Senzie, according to John Knox, is taken from the old Scots word meaning Synod; the fair lasted two weeks and was held on the Monday after Easter), and, up to the 1920s the East Fife Unionists held their garden parties and fêtes on the same grounds of the then Priory House. This mansion house—once the property of the Crichton-Stuart family of Falkland, and latterly a home for evacuees—was demolished after World War II.

11. St Andrews Palace-Castle from the south-east showing the courtyard with the remains of the Sea Tower (centre), the Kitchen Tower (right) and the 14th century Fore Tower (left).

12. An ex-baker from Anstruther, Alex George Butters (b.1822), was appointed 'Castle Keeper' in 1893.

13. Dick Martin, the modern-day castle custodian.

The presence of the Augustinians in St Andrews was to be very significant for the town's future prominence. They came to St Andrews from the then mother house of the order at Scone, under the auspices of Bishop Robert, a Norman-Frenchman who had been a former prior of Scone. The first prior of the Augustinian clergy at St Andrews cathedral was appointed in 1144, and thereafter these men administered the cathedral for the bishop and carried out the duties of their order within the cathedral chapter. No extended records of the priory have survived, but undoubtedly the prior acted as dean of the cathedral. In time the priory of St Andrews had dependencies at Loch Leven (Portmoak), Monymusk and Pittenweem.

Taking as their guidance the Rule of St Augustine of Hippo (354-430), derived from his fourth century writings, the Augustinians of St Andrews lived a communal life within a community much as in a monastery, but *not* as monks—they were ordained clergy doing pastoral work. They were called Canons Regular—Black Canons to distinguish them from the Premonstratensian Canons (White Canons)—and their dress was a black cloak, distinctive rochet and biretta. A 13th century monastic chronicler, Guyot de Provens, said of them: 'The Augustine rule is more courteous than that of Benedict. Among them one is well shod, well clothed, and well fed. They go out when they like, mix with the world and talk at table.' The prior became mitred in 1418 (a symbol of the increased authority of the foundation and the 'cloven tongues' of the apostolic commission, *Acts* 2.3.)

The duties of the Augustinians within the town were to carry out the diocesan policy of their Bishop Superior; they administered the church of the Holy Trinity and 'taught' within Fife. Levels of literacy varied amongst these clergy from the university graduate to the scarcely literate, although the majority of the local Augustinians would be classed as 'gentry'. Their church duties would be the singing of Divine Office—the service of prayer and praise, psalms, lessons, hymns, ancillary and distinct fom the sacrifice of the Mass. Usually the Canons Regular would have a personal devotion each day of some one and a half hours; to this they added their work for the active apostolate. Great days for the Canons Regular would be the Feasts of St Andrew, 28th August, St Michael the Archangel, 29th September (Michaelmas), and St Margaret of Scotland, 10th June, when all the canons would be required to conduct Mass either in the cathedral or within the churches of Fife. In any case the canons would follow the services of the monastic day. According to the seasons this would be the range of worship in the cathedral, with the main meal of

14. St Andrews castle contains a very rare example of medieval siege
warfare, a mine and counter-mine. Tunnelled through the rock, they
date from the Franco-Scottish siege of the Protestant adherents of
1546-47.

15. For centuries the Kitchen Tower, the work of a prelate, Bishop Walter Trail (1385-1401), has been buffeted by the raging tides of St Andrews Bay.

the day at noon in summer and 2.00 pm in winter. At 2.00 am they would rise, at 2.15-2.30 am prayers were conducted with psalms and Matins (the first service of the day) followed by Lauds; Dawn would see the service of Prime and private reading in the cloister. 8.00 am would give time for a wash, a light breakfast and the service of Tierce and Morrow Mass. 9.00 am was registered as the Chapter meeting (the everyday administration of the priory was discussed here) with work within the cathedral or priory and a further reading time. Noon saw the sequence of services of Sext, High Mass, Nones followed by Dinner. At 2.30 pm there would be more reading and work for those canons within the cathedral and priory (others may have been out on 'missions'). At 5.00 pm came the service of Vespers and Supper. Compline, the last service of the day, came at 6.00pm and bed at 7.00pm. The bell for all prayers would be rung by the canon appointed as sub-sacristan, and at the door leading from the night stair would sit the *circa*, the canon who noted if anyone had overslept, was absent or late. Some of the canons would be excused the services of the day if they had to carry out pastoral or claustral duties. There would be a number of laity employed in the cathedral and priory to do the cleaning, cooking and chores of the daily routines.

The prior had a staff of ten main 'lieutenants'. The *sacristan* looked after the church fabric and holy vessels, and was responsible for the cathedral security (the main dangers were fire and burglary). The *precentor* (chanter) assessed the music and books; the *infirmarian* tended the sick; the *almoner* cared for the poor; the *hospitaler* (guestmaster) looked after travellers; the *cellarer* was in charge of the food, drink and stores; the *kitchener* directed all the cooking arrangements; the *refectorian* saw to the charge of the dining room; the *pittancer* supervised the 'extra' dishes of the meals for special religious holidays; and the *chamberlain* took charge of the clothing and bedding. Because of its prominence St Andrews cathedral would have an income of around £12,500 a year to fund its administration.

The diocesan administration was complete with the installation of an archdeacon (once called 'the bishop's eye') at what is now Deanscourt. This was the Archdeacon's Manse and was reconstructed around 1570 by Sir George Douglas, whose coat of arms can be seen above the modern gateway. The property passed into the ownership of Sir John Spottiswoode of Dairsie in 1622 and had various occupants until in 1953 the university authorities started alterations (for instance, they re-opened the gateway which had been blocked up for years and set within it an ornamental gate.) Today the building is a residence for some fifty research students, having been set apart for this purpose in 1951.

Denominationally St Andrews today is immovably Presbyterian, and four churches of the 'Church of Scotland' persuasion form the bulk of the total congregation. Of the four, Hope Park Church is the oldest 'modern' foundation. Its originators were the early seceders from the established church (after the Reformation), and the original meeting-place was a barn in one of the 'closes' off South Street known as Imrie's Close. Here from 1749 to 1774 the seceders (Burgher Kirk) worshipped. Then they moved to North Street and ultimately they opened their new church in 1865. The congregation was variously known as the Burghers, the United Session, the United Presbytarian, the United Free, until in 1929 they entered the fold of the 'Church of Scotland'. Martyrs Church, North Street, was the next in foundation and opened in 1844 to be renovated in 1852; in 1928 it was rebuilt. St Leonard's Parish Church in Hepburn Gardens was opened in 1904, and the reconstructed Holy Trinity was opened in 1909.

The Victorian Baptist Church was 'improved' in 1901-02, and the Roman Catholic Church of St James was built in 1910. Before, the Roman Catholics worshipped in an iron shelter which dated from 1884-85. From the Reformation, Catholicism went 'underground', and when Episcopacy was abolished in 1689 the devout Episcopalians were forced to worship in secret in houses within the town. Anyone caught letting Episcopalians worship in his house was fined, as was Margaret Skinner of 42 South Street. As greater tolerance evolved the 'piscies' were allowed to worship in peace (their support of the Jacobites had not done their religious freedom any good) and they opened a chapel in North Street in 1825. Today the Episcopalians have two churches, All Saints in North Castle Street (1923) and St Andrew's, Queen's Gardens; the latter was built 1867-69, but its tower was demolished in 1939. A mission church for fisherfolk was started in 1903 on the present site of All Saints Church; this church was extended in 1907 and earned the name of 'the bundle kirk' by the fisherfolk because of the charity parcels made up and distributed by the congregation.

To be Archbishop of St Andrews was to rule a realm within a realm from Kincardine to Lothian. The archbishop had command over the spiritual and secular aspects of many lives, and his representatives were all-seeing and had no doors closed to them. The archbishop, too, was at the head of two administrative systems; one was ecclesiastical, operating through the diocesan apparatus, while the other was temporal, through which he administered the diocesan lands. He had involvement too in the priory of St Andrews, whose canons formed the archbishop's chapter, the work of his eight suffragan bishops—Dunkeld, Brechin, Dunblane, Aberdeen, Caithness, Orkney, Moray and Ross—and the university of St Andrews, of which he was Chancellor. Indeed, as primate of all Scotland he was able to mould policy both in questions of politics and religion, which was as far reaching (and in some cases more so) as the power of the monarch.

The archbishop's household was enormous, and like the university today he was the biggest employer in the town. Many plum jobs were allocated through nepotism, but the archbishop employed a wide range of local people, from the young laird of Kellie to artisans living in the town. The archbishop's retinue was calculated in hundreds and ranged from gunners and masons, to cooks and musicians, and from French body servants and brewers, to tailors and apothecaries.

St Andrews castle, as we see it today, is composed principally of stonework which dates from the 16th century. Chronicles record that the first castle here was erected *circa* 1200 by Bishop Roger, principally as a residence for himself and his successors. Before this the bishops had lived within the priory. So, from the start, the castle was intimately associated with the cathedral's nobility. Bishop William de Malvoisine probably completed the first phase of the building when he succeeded in 1202. The castle forms an irregular pentagon and its rôle in Scottish history has been as an episcopal and archiepiscopal palace, a fortress and as a state prison.

Severally in the hands of the Scots and the English, the castle figured in all the nation's wars and followed a pattern of being raised and rebuilt, expanded and repaired, right up to the work of the last great builder, Archbishop John Hamilton (1549-71), who erected the present frontal range. Once, the castle had two massive circular blockhouses at the southeast and southwest corners of the frontage; these vanished in the bombardment of 1546-47.

The castle had many famous visitors: James III, Scotland's intellectual king, with his unconventional interests in crafts and sciences, was born here in 1451; and James IV was a frequent visitor. Perhaps the castle's zenith of splendour came with the two Beatons, uncle and nephew. Archbishop James Beaton

16. The corner tower, or 'Roundel' of 1 South St. with its distinctive balustraded parapet. This is an important three-storeyed house, with a panel (from an earlier building) on the east gable, bearing the arms of Prior Haldenstone (1418-43).

18.   The eastern aspect of North St, medieval Northgait, from St Salvator's Tower.

17.   *(facing page)* Modern demolition has revealed the cathedral precinct wall in Abbey St.

19.   South St. at its junction with Bell St. in the 1930s. The railings around the Madras College were removed as a part of metals collection during World War II.

(1523-39) maintained such a lavish hospitality that it was thus described by the English ambassador: 'I understand there hath not been such a house kept in Scotland many days before, as of late the said archbishop hath kept, and yet keepeth; insomuch as at the being with him of these lords (Angus, Lennox Argyle etc), both horses and men, he gave livery nightly to twenty-one score horses.'

James Beaton (the last archbishop to be buried in the cathedral) was succeeded by his nephew, the famous Cardinal David Beaton (1539-46). A man of strong Roman Catholic ambitions, Beaton's zeal for orthodoxy led him to prosecute and persecute heretics, and his most celebrated (and, best-remembered) victim was George Wishart (born *circa*. 1513). A native of Angus, Wishart was charged with heresy because he had taught the New Testament in Greek. After study in Germany, Switzerland and at Corpus Christi, Cambridge, he returned to Scotland in 1543 as part of that English envoy bent on urging Henry VIII's scheme to marry Mary Queen of Scots to the infant Prince Edward. Wishart's preaching, despite Knox's exoneration, was political and religious rabble-rousing, but heresy was the charge, not political plotting, and he was burned outside the castle on 1st March, 1546. The initials 'G.W.' are set in the roadway outside the castle to mark the site of the martyrdom.

The death of Wishart was one of the elements in the conspiracy which led to Beaton's murder at the castle on 29th May, 1546; after which his body was displayed naked and suspended from a window of one of the now vanished blockhouses. Beaton's death produced two great changes; the omnipotent power of the Roman Catholic Church was entombed with him in the convent of the Black Friars, and St Andrews was never again the centre of government, or political skullduggery.

After the rebuilding of the castle by Archbishop Hamilton the fabric was beseiged no more, and there began a long series of ownerships. During the Presbyterian ascendancy, in 1587 an Act of Annexation transferred the castle (along with the other church property) to the Crown. By a charter dated 1st July 1606, the castle was granted to George, Earl of Dunbar. It reverted to the (Episcopal) Archbishop of St Andrews in 1612, but was irregularly used as a residence. The office of Constable of St Andrews Castle fell into desuetude as the importance of the castle diminished. In 1654 the St Andrews Town Council ordered part of the stone to be used to repair the harbour wall, and by 1685 the castle was considered a 'hopeless ruin'. The moat was cleaned out in 1864-65 by order of Provost Playfair, and the castle continued as a popular 'view'. In 1911 the castle passed into the hands of the state, and today is held in trust for the nation by the Secretary of State for Scotland and is cared for by the Scottish Development Department, as are the cathedral and the priory ruins.

Two facets of the castle which continually fascinate visitors are the 'Bottle Dungeon' and the countermines. Situated in the Sea Tower, at the northwest part of the castle, is a prison cell in whose floor is set a 24ft deep pit known as the 'Bottle Dungeon', on account of its shape. Protestants and Black Friars alike suffered in the pit which is perhaps the most incompassionate of all Scottish prisons.

20.   South St., medieval Southgait, exhibits a fine series of 16th and 17th century mansions at its eastern end, some with fine Georgian features.

21.   The most complete close now left in St Andrews, Louden's Close, with its pantiled houses, displays renovation work of the Preservation Trust of 1941 and 1949.

22.   The east end of Market St., medieval Mercatgait, with the memorial fountain to George John Whyte-Melville (1821-78), the Victorian novelist.

23. Market St. as it was c.1936; in the distance is the tower of **Hope Park Church** (1864).

24. The Town House, Market St., c.1860, which was demolished in 1862, after the erection of the new municipal buildings opened in South St. in July 1861.

25. Two banks overlook the cobbled east end of Market St.; the Royal Bank of Scotland was opened in 1857 and the Bank of Scotland in 1971 (on the site of the British Linen Bank, 1903).

26. Once a boundary of land owned by Sir William Lindsay and the site of a medieval cemetery, modern Logie's Lane (once 'Wynd') displays both modern and ancient architecture in juxtaposition.

27. Portrayal of the interior of a Victorian grocery shop in St Andrews within the Preservation Trust Museum, North St. Above is displayed the 1905 lettering of the prestigious grocery establishment of Messrs Aikman and Terras, established c.1847 by Andrew Aikman Sr.

The mines and countermines are a rare example of medieval seige technique and were tunnelled through the rock during the seige of 1546-47. At that time the Protestants held the castle aided and abetted by Henry VIII of England, and were beseiged by a Franco-Scottish force acting under the regency of Marie de Guise-Lorraine. The purpose of the tunnelling was to undermine the fortifications; the countermines were begun by the defenders to thwart these moves. The entrance to the beseigers' mine is underneath the modern house, at the corner of Castle Wynd, while the countermine is entered from within the precincts of the castle. These mines gave rise to the Victorian myths about 'secret passages' leading to the cathedral. One of the promoters of these tall stories was former Dean of Guild W.T. Linskill (1855-1929) who fondly believed that there was a set of 'secret steps' to be found somewhere in the cathedral, at the bottom of which was a cache where the priests had hidden the cathedral treasures from the mob.

There are those who believe that, although the castle has not been inhabited for 300 years, there are 'other inhabitants' still there today. The street lamps, the nocturnal flutterings of owls, the moonlight through gun-embrasures, all give rise to 'ghostly' *trompe l'oeil,* but there are residents and visitors willing enough to lay their credibility on the line to aver that they saw a castle ghost. Two such were students at the university.

At 12.30 am on 1st March, 1983 (the anniversary of the martyrdom of George Wishart), Elizabeth Doctor, of Broughty Ferry, and Mary Mohr of Lake Forrest, Illinois, scaled the wall between the ruined castle and Castlecliffe. For a while they walked around the moonlight-flooded castle sward and walked slowly towards the front of the castle. To their horror the girls saw, in the right hand window of the remaining square tower, a beckoning arm high up in the stonework. A head and a neck-shape appeared and disappeared, and the sequence was repeated several times over a period of five minutes. The girls are convinced that the appearance was not of rational explanation . . . a fluttering bird, a trick of the light . . . and they scuttled away in a state of terror.

Today the castle calls to mind a function which also shows the prominence of the town in past times, for at the castle were kept the dies and punches of the bishops' coiners.

Once bishops were men of power, whose influence was felt far beyond the boundaries of their diocese. St Andrews history is particularly marked with the ecclesiastical puissance of bishops who fought in wars, founded universities, and amassed wealth far beyond the scope of their holy work. One such was our Bishop Kennedy (*circa.* 1408-65). Kennedy took a prominent part in the politics of Scotland during the minority of King James II, and afterwards acted as regent during the minority of King James III. Once one of Scotland's famous councillors, James Kennedy was thus described by an old chronicle: He was 'wondrous godlie and wise, weill learned in divine services, and in the civill lawis.' Above all he had a rare privilege: he was granted permission to mint coins. Today these coins are much sought after by private collectors and museums.

28. Once called Mercat Wynd, College St. is now closed to vehicular traffic and takes its name from the college founded by Bishop James Kennedy. Several of the two-storey pantiled houses have been renovated.

29.
cathedral from St Salvator's
Tower, in the distance to the right rise
Kinkell Braes and the coastal walk to Crail.

Before 1919 few examples were known of the copper pennies and farthings of Bishop Kennedy's mint—probably sited at St Andrews castle. A chance find threw more light on this clerical coiner and started a wrangle amongst historians. In 1919, amongst the débris choking the bed of the stream which had been used to flush the latrines in the Corrodiar's Houses and the Abbot's lodgings, was found a large number of coins in the Abbey of Crossraguel in South Ayrshire. An off-shoot of Cluniac (the Black Monks of Cluny in France) Abbey at Paisley, Crossraguel had been founded in 1244 and subsequent ages had brought the Abbot many privileges making him a very powerful man.

At first the prominence of the Abbot of Crossraguel led scholars to believe that the coins found had been minted there. Coins of an original and private design, of course, would have to have had, at the very least, a royal warrant. This warrant would have been even more important if the 'Crossraguel coins' were to circulate freely in Scotland and be accepted in areas where the abbot and his establishment were totally unknown. A search of the papers and royal charters of the abbey, such as those of Robert I (1324) and Robert III (1404), produced no evidence that the abbot had been licensed as a coiner.

'What cleric at the time had power to mint?' scholars asked. The answer was easy to find . . . James Kennedy, Bishop of St Andrews! It was found by researchers that Bishop Kennedy had been granted by a charter the privilege of striking coins, by James II on 14 June 1452.

30. North St., c.1860, showing the former site of St Andrews Episcopal Church, now situated in Queen's Terrace where it was consecrated on 8th April 1869. The old building seen in the picture was sold to the Free Church congregation in Buckhaven, the stones being dismantled and shipped by sea. Herein was to be found the original building called College Gate (the home of Col. W.H. McLaren, C.O. of the 1st Royal Dragoons) which gave its name to the present site.

31. North St. and College Gate as they are today.

32. Modern shop fronts on the south side of Market St. The removal of tax on sheet and plate glass in 1846 led to the great changes in the town's shop fronts.

33. An unusually traffic-free scene in Church St. which takes its name from Holy Trinity Church. The Music Shop was originally Alexander Fyfe's Hardware and Fancy Goods Emporium and sported a fine fascia by the St Andrews architect, James Scott (1861-1944).

34. Lady Lilias Graham, daughter of the 7th Duke of Montrose, kinswoman of the famous 5th Earl and 1st Marquess, signatory of the National Covenant, 1638.

35. Medal of James Graham, 5th Earl and 1st Marquess of Montrose, 1628. Having won the archery contest that year, he was privileged to hang the medal on the silver arrow he had won. Archery was popular in the university in the 17th and 18th centuries and there were competitions from 1618; usually they were held in March at the Bow Butts. The competitions were revived by the Kate Kennedy Club in the form of a Scottish Archery Association Competition.

> Nomina incorporatorum et jurantium in religionis articulos, et Academiæ Leges 26 Ianuarij 1627 e' Collegio Salvatoriano Rectore Roberto Howæo SS Th. D. et Collegij Mariani præfecto: Regente M. Gulielmo Martino
>
> Joannes Gordonius Comes Sutherlandiæ.
> Jacobus Gramus Comes Montereuse.

36. Page from the Matriculation Register of the University showing the signature of James Graham (1612-50) who succeeded his father in 1626 as Marquess of Montrose. Montrose was at St Salvator's College 1627-29.

37. *(facing page)* The tower of St Salvator's College, 1450.

There were 51 pennies and 88 farthings of the 'Kennedy/St Andrews' type discovered at Crossraguel. Of the general type, the pennies bear on the obverse an orb with a cross breaking through the legend to act as a mintmark. This is surrounded by royal titles; *Iacobus Dei Gra(tia) Rex*—'James, by the Grace of God, King'. On the reverse a Latin cross in a tressure of four arcs, with the motto *Crux Pellit Omne Crimen,* the first line of the vesper hymn *Ante Somnum,* by Prudentius. Compared with the coins of today the issues look very rough and badly struck.

The first variety of the 'Kennedy/St Andrews' farthings was copied in part from the second issue 'black farthings' of James III, which had appeared in the early 1470s. The reverse design is quite original, bearing a long cross pattée with six-pointed mullets and crowns in alternate angles: the reverse inscription reads *Mone(ta) Paup(erum),* or 'money of the poor'.

The reverse of the second variety of these coins is similar, but the cross has floreated ends and the mullets are of five points and occupy all quarters of the cross. The new obverse shows a large trefoil, with a mullet in the centre, a *fleur-de-lis* in each leaf, and a crown in the two outer angles above. The third variety only differs in having the words abbreviated to *Mo Pauper.* The designs of Kennedy's coins can compare closely with the work on the mace of St Salvator's College. The coins of Bishop Kennedy had a wide circulation in the east of Scotland, and are a rare treasure for they form the only medieval coins of the whole of Great Britain not only to have been struck by the authority of a primate, but which bear his own arms. Bishop Kennedy was the only ecclesiastic whose issues did not conform exactly to regal issues. It is interesting to note that coins were minted in St Andrews under Alexander III (1241-86) and John Baliol (1250-1313), the former bearing the name of Thomas the Minter and the latter the name of the town, boldly and clearly.

In medieval times Scottish burghs were graded by rank. They consisted of cities, or burghs possessing a cathedral; Royal Burghs, which were created by the monarch of the day; Burghs of Regality, and Burghs of Barony, which lay within the estate of a high church official, or titled landowner, and these were the creation of a bishop, a peer, or a laird. St Andrews was thus a Burgh of Barony being a 'bishop's burgh' at first, but was to become a Royal Burgh, and the date of the actual foundation is a matter of dispute. Nevertheless it was Bishop Robert (1126-59) who first gave the town prominence. The 'Extract of Matriculation of the Arms of the City of Saint Andrews' (1912) records that in the reign of David I (1124-53) the town was elected into a Royal Burgh (the date 1140 is suggested) with Maynard the Fleming, a mason and a burgess of Berwick-upon-Tweed, as its first provost (*praefectus*). In reality St Andrews was founded as a Bishop's Burgh by leave of David I somewhere between 1124 and 1144. In 1614 it was made a Burgh of Regality under the Archbishop of St Andrews, and James VI made the town a Royal Burgh in 1620. (It must be realised that St Andrews was a *de facto* Royal Burgh much earlier).

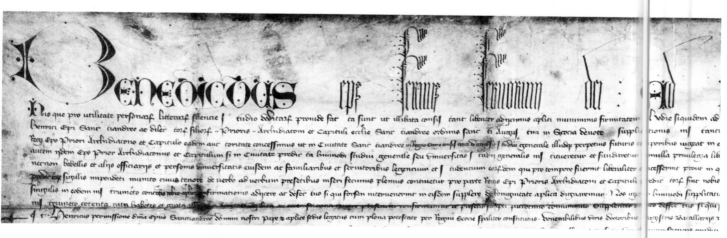

38. The Foundation Bull of the University, granted by Pope Benedict XIII in August 1413, confirmed the Charter of Incorporation from Bishop Henry Wardlaw. The text begins: 'Benedict, the bishop, servant of the servants of God . . .'

The administrative heart of the burgh was in Market Street whose west end housed the old Tolbooth, demolished in 1862, and the Mercat Cross and Tron, or public weighbeam, removed in 1768. The present Town Hall, no longer in use since the local government reorganistion, was formerly opened in 1861. When the Rev. Dr John Adamson, first Minister of St Andrews, gave his return on St Andrews to Sir John Sinclair for his *Statistical Account of Scotland* 1791-99, the Royal Burgh of St Andrews was governed by a Provost, Dean of Guild and Town Treasurer and four baillies, who were elected by the council every Michaelmas. A council, made up of 29 members representing the deacons, crafts and guilds of the town, ruled the burgh. Today St Andrews, in terms of local government, is in the North East Fife District. This came about in 1975 with the disastrous (for the rights and interests of the people of St Andrews) re-organisation of local government and the Administration and Council headquarters are in the former Fife County Buildings, at Cupar. St Andrews is also represented by a Community Council which purports to be 'The eyes, ears and voice of the citizens of St Andrews'. In reality it is a toothless 'talking-shop' which the citizens treat with growing apathy.

The 'treasures' of the former Royal Burgh of St Andrews are kept at the Town Hall. The chain of office worn by the provosts was presented to the burgh in 1897 by John-Patrick Crichton-Stuart (1847-1900), the 3rd Marquess of Bute. St Andrews only had a full-time Town Clerk from 1948, and the last provost was J. B. Gilchrist who served 1973-75. A chain for the wife of the provost to wear on civic occasions was presented by Mrs Georgina Fordyce, wife of T. T. Fordyce, draper, who was three times provost of the burgh.

From 1707 to the 1832 Reform Act, St Andrews was combined with Forfar, Cupar, Perth and Dundee to share one Member of Parliament. After the passing of the 1832 Act, St Andrews Burgh came into being to include Cupar, Crail, Anstruther Easter, Anstruther Wester, Kilrenny and Pittenweem. The first M.P. for the new constituency was Andrew Johnson Jr., a Liberal listed as 'A Reformer, in favour of the immediate abolition of slavery . . .' The Liberals continued to hold the seat and in 1885 Sir Robert Anstruther changed the political complexion to Liberal Unionist. The Reform Act of 1918 brought St Andrews Burghs into the East Fife Constituency and a poltical turmoil was achieved when Col. Sir A. Sprot, the Unionist, defeated the ex-Liberal Prime Minister H. H. Asquith (1852-1928). The Liberal soon won the seat back and the only other real ripple in the political water was in the form of the East Fife By-Election of 1933 caused by the death of James Duncan Millar, the Liberal representative. The seat was won by J. Henderson Stewart for the Conservatives and by and large the Conservatives (as Conservative Liberal Unionists, or National Liberal & Conservatives) have represented St Andrews in parliament ever since, but with a decreasing majority within the East Fife constituency.

Changes came too among the St Andrews townsfolk who were eligible to vote. Under the 1832 Act those persons who were occupiers of homes of £10 clear value, whether as proprietor, tenant, life-renter, or joint-occupier, with the non-resident true owners, or similar premises, and husbands *Jure uxoris* after the death of their wives, holding by the courtesy of Scotland, were allowed to vote. The Representation of the People (Scotland) Act 1868 brought Scotland in line with the new franchise for England and Wales, but fixed the property qualification for county occupiers at £14 instead of £12, per year. The Act of 1884 created a uniform householder and lodger franchise in every borough and county in the United Kingdom. Those who had lands, or tenements, worth £10 a year were also franchised. By the Act of 1918 the radical principle of 'one man one vote' was enacted except for the university voters and owners of business premises. Women had to be over 30 to vote and be property owners in their own right, or through husbands; this was 'regularised' in 1928 when Stanley Baldwin's Conservative government gave the vote to all women over 21.

In Scotland two new universty seats were created by the 1867 Reform Act and St Andrews was grouped with Edinburgh. Those eligible to vote were the Chancellors, the members of the University Courts, professors, and members of the General Council. The first M.P. to represent Edinburgh and St Andrews was (Sir) Hugh Lyon Playfair, who served from 1868-85 as a Liberal. The first Conservative to win was the Rt. Hon. J. H. A. Macdonald who served from 1885-88; thereafter the Conservatives (as Unionists, Liberal Unionists, Conservative Unionists) predominated. Later the two university seats were combined to represent four universities (St Andrews, Aberdeen, Glasgow and Edinburgh) with three M.P.s, and described as the Scottish Universities constituencies, balloted for by Proportional Representation. The university seats were abolished by the Representation of the People Act 1948 and no longer appeared after the February 1950 election.

During the boom years of the 12th century the basic structure of the layout of the town was achieved and this has not changed in seven hundred years. In fact, only one street has altered out of all recognition

39. Now called the West Port, 'Southgait Port', is the only surviving town gateway. As seen today it was built in 1589 and modelled on the Edinburgh Netherbow Port; it was extensively renovated 1843-45, when the side arches were added.

40. *(facing page)* Lammas Fair, the oldest surviving medieval market in Scotland. At the turn of the century it was a hiring fair

IN · PRINCIPIO · ERAT · VERBVM

41. The gateway of St Mary's College (founded 1537). The coat of arms incorporates the heraldic devices of Archbishop James Beaton and Archbishop John Hamilton, with the *fleur-de-lis* representing the original dedication to the Blessed Mary of the Assumption. The motto is from St John's Gospel, 1.1., 'In the beginning was the Word'.

James Murray, janitor, with fan-tailed doves at St Mary's College.

43. Head janitor at St Salvator's and Bedellus, John McCartney, with the 15th century Mace of the Faculty of Canon Law.

and that is Abbey Street (old Prior's Wynd) which was widened, with many houses demolished, after World War II. So, the three main streets radiated westwards from the great west door of the cathedral and probably followed age-old tracks linking *Cendrigmonaid* with the Pictish hinterland.

North Street (once Northgait) and South Street (Southgait), with Market Street (Mercatgait) and its narrow extension to the east (Narrow Mercatgait) were well-established with dwellings by medieval times. The two Castle Streets were formerly Rattonrow and Fishergate, and linked South Street with the castle precinct wall (Castlegait), and its extension westwards, The Scores (Swallowgait). A 16th century panoramic view of St Andrews shows The Scores virtually uninhabited, but the four gateways into the burgh are clearly marked. The northernmost gateway was set in The Scores at the end of Castlegait; the North Street gateway was approximately in line with modern Murray Park; the Mercatgait gateway was at the end of modern Bell Street/Greyfriars Garden abutting the 15th century house of the Franciscan Friars destroyed by the Reformers. The only surviving gateway is the West Port (Southgait Port). The land within the town was apportioned by dwelling, and running out from South Street were the 'lang rigges' on the southern-sloping ridge leading down to the Kinness Burn, on which the burgesses grew kail and grazed cattle. Several of the prominent guildsmen and merchants developed their plots as ornamental gardens. The abundant springs along the ridge fed the house wells and South Street was a favourite area of the wealthy for a very long time. St Andrews was never a 'walled city' like York, or Chester, and the most fortified area was undoubtedly the castle precincts.

Stackyards, cattlesheds and pigsties were all seen in the centre of St Andrews less than one hundred years ago. The town has had many changing phases of architectural development, and has hit some ecological lows. One such nadir was in 1697 when it was proposed to transfer the university to Perth. A contemporary chronicle thus records the state of the town: 'This place being now only a village, where most part farmers dwell, the whole streets are filled with dunghills, which are exceedingly noisome and ready to infect the air, especially at this season *Autumn,* when the herring guts are exposed in them, or rather in all corners of the town by themselves; and the season of the year apt to breed infection, which partly may be said to have been the occasion of last year's dysenterie, and which from its beginning here, raged through most part of the kingdom.'

44. Dating in its present aspect from P. Macgregor Chalmers's 'renovation' of 1907-09, the 'Town Kirk' of Holy Trinity was founded in 1410-12 by Henry Wardlaw, Bishop of St Andrews. In 1799 Wardlaw's church (which itself replaced a parish church sited behind the east gable of the cathedral) was almost totally pulled down; only the bartizan tower, which predominates this picture is of 15th century date. Holy Trinity was the pro-cathedral of three arch-bishops of which the most famous was the murdered Archbishop James Sharp (1618-79) whose tomb is to be found in the south tran-sept. The famed weather-cock was taken down in 1866. The Citizen Bookshop at 107 South Street is the work of the architect Frank Pride and dates from 1928.

This decay was to last for almost one hundred and fifty years when in 1830 it was further described: 'The streets were irregular and most inconvenient; many of the recent accesses to the various quarters, such as North and South Bell Streets, Playfair Terrace, and so forth, were then unbuilt; there was not a foot of side pavement in any of the streets; filth and squalor abounded unchecked; cows and pigs grazed in front of the colleges; the venerable ruins were fast going to decay, and were littered with rubbish; the lines of the public streets were continually broken by awkward abutments of ungainly houses; there were few visitors of any distinction even to the splendid links, which lay with all its vast capabilities almost untrodden; and generally, St Andrews, considering the prestige of its antiquity as an ecclesiastical capital, and its rank as a seat of learning, was at the lowest pitch of miserable neglect and decay.'

Definite steps were taken to redevelop the town and expansion plans were carried out. Beyond the West Port was the ancient settlement of Argyle, where handloom weaving once predominated, made up of modern Argyle Street (1843) and John Street (1869) running parallel with Double Dykes Road (Aberdouncy Gait). Between their ends ran the Cowgait (now City road) leading to the cow pastures and the town windmill (as remembered in modern Windmill Road), and linking with the extension of North Street, called Rogergait (now Pilmour Links and Pilmour Place). Old guidebooks of St Andrews speak of breweries situated in the town and one business eventually established itself in Argyle Street. Provost John Wilson (d.1938) came to St Andrews in 1877 and set up an aereated water factory first in South Street, then in Market Street. He purchased the brewery of D.S. Ireland Ltd in 1902 and set up the premises of John Wilson & Co (the vaults of the firm went back to the 18th century). Today the site has become a controversial issue as a possible redevelopment area. Incidentally the Argyle Brewery has one of the deepest wells in Scotland. The bore goes down 225 ft and was sunk by Largo miners in the late 1880s; the well is 160 ft below sea-level.

The only way to expand was west and south, and terraced buildings began to develop like Playfair Terrace (1846) and Gibson Place (1858-71). One particularly interesting development was the 'garden square' of Howard Place, Hope Street and Abbotsford Crescent. These three streets were begun in 1849 and form three terraces, one straight, one concave, and one convex. The inspiration was undoubtedly Edinburgh's New Town. The gardens remain private and are administered by a committee of residents. This scheme was the inspiration of James Hope, a parliamentary barrister, who saw in the growth of golfing a need to build streets of 'gentlemen's houses'. Towards this end he bought the land known as Sir John Gladstone's Park. Abbotsford Crescent now makes up the mixed residence of John & Eliza McIntosh Hall. The nucleus of the building was bequeathed by Professor W.C.McIntosh in 1931 as a memorial to his parents. The names of the streets, and nearby Lockhart Place which adjoins, are interesting in their literary associations. James Robert Hope Q.C., married Charlotte Lockhart, the daughter of John Gibson Lockhart (1794-1854), Scottish man of letters, himself the son-in-law of Sir Walter Scott (1771-1832). Abbotsford Crescent was named after Sir Walter's home in the Borders. James Hope married (Charlotte died in 1858) secondly Lady Victoria Fitzalan Howard, so that the street names were now complete. To the south of South Street, Queens Gardens (1862-64) was developed through to Queens Terrace (1865) and Dempster Terrace (1871).

By the mid-1850s the well-heeled *rentiers* began to erect mock-Baronial edifices of which Kinburn, Edgecliffe and Westerlea are fine examples. Hepburn Gardens, Kennedy Gardens and Buchanan Gardens were logical developments to the west. The bulk of the houses across the Kinness Burn are 'municpal schemes' and were developed from the first Town Council scheme of 1925. Greenside Place was re-developed in 1932 to link this 'little town' to the south with the main town.

Today the town still sports some interesting examples of architectural designs of the 1920s and 1930s, for example the 'Citizen' shop (1929), the Picture House (1931) and the Abattoir (1933). During the 1930s St Andrews Town Council enacted a series of civic vandalisms which were irreversible. They tore down medieval houses which did not meet with prevailing housing standards. Not even private money to restore the houses to their former glory was countenanced, making the councillors worthy ancestors of Knox's mob who destroyed Scotland's medieval heritage.

The St Andrews Preservation Trust Ltd was founded in 1937 'to preserve for the benefit of the public the amenities and historic character of the City and Royal Burgh of St Andrews and of its neighbourhood,' and does sterling work in preserving among other things properties and antiques, costume and photographic material. The work of the Trust was greatly enhanced by the development of a Museum at 12 North Street. A major problem with the Trust, however, is the rapidly increasing age range of its most enthusiastic members; the Trust needs to make great efforts in putting the preservation of the town's history over to the young people of the area, otherwise 'preservation' as a concept has no future . . . in many ways this would be a very fine joint-venture for both town and gown groups.

45. St Mary's College, founded in 1537, is the college where
Divinity is taught. The aged thorn tree at the foot of the bell-
tower is said to have been planted by Mary Queen of Scots.
To the left of the picture is a part of the massive holm oak
tree.

46. The silver of St Mary's College. Seen here (l. to r.) are: the Silver Tassie, or Guild Cup, London hallmark 1613, presented by Principal Wm. Guild of King's College, Aberdeen, 1628. The Capstan Salt Dish was used when St Mary's was a Residential College. It has the St Andrews hallmark, a Saltire Cross, and the initials of the maker Patrick Gairdin, 1670. The Mazer, or Drinking Cup, or Common Cup was used for wines. Dated 1563, it is the oldest piece of silver with the Edinburgh hallmark. Made of silver and walnut, it has a trumpet stem and carries punches of the maker, Alexander Auchinleck. The translations of the inscriptions inside the Mazer read thus:

1 John ch. 1 v. 17

'For the law was given by Moses but Grace & Truth came by Jesus Christ'.

1Corinthians ch. 10 v. 31

'Whether therefore ye eat, or drink or whatsoever ye do—do all to the Glory of God'.

Modern assessors believe that the Mazer could be older than inscribed.

If it had not been for the university, the only survivor of the great medieval ecclesiastical foundations, St Andrews today might have been no more than a decayed fishing village struggling to be a middle-class dormitory for Dundee, as the Industrial Revolution did not reach the burgh. Before the establishment of the university, the monastery of the Culdees at Kirk Hill would have had a brief to teach and study the gospels. That brief was absorbed by the Augustianian priests of the priory, who became natural heirs to the developing need for a university. It is without a doubt that teaching was established within the priory long before the coming of the university.

Real change was to effect the University of St Andrews in four main ways. The 16th century saw the infiltration of Renaissance ideas to the university and the reshaping of its teachings by the Protestant Reformers. The university developed, from a theological standpoint, in the 17th century, through a period of narrow and dogmatic educational democracy into intellectual regressiveness. Both the Calvinists and the Episcopalians of the period brought their own turgid semantics developed out of their own fanaticisms. The 18th century was an 'Age of Enlightenment' within the university, leading to the marked reorganisation of the university with Victorian thoroughness.

St Andrews University did not have a single date of foundation, and its origins can be spread over a period of four years. In 1410 it is known that a group of academics, mostly graduates from the 13th century university at Paris, inaugurated a school of higher education within the town. Two years later these scholars had so established themselves that they obtained a charter of incorporation with privileges from the diocesan bishop, Henry Wardlaw (*circa.* 1372-1440). During August 1413, this charter was confirmed and extended by a series of Papal Bulls (an edict of the Pope with his seal affixed, from the Latin *bulla,* a leaden seal), promulgated in 1414, so by that date the university was formally in existence.

In all there were six Papal Bulls associated with the new university, of which the most important was the 'Bull of Foundation'. The Bulls were confirmed by Cardinal Peter de Luna (1328-1423), known to history as the Avignon anti-pope Benedict XIII. The Bulls founding the university were brought to St Andrews by Henry Ogilvie, a priest of the diocese, and arrived on Saturday, 3rd February, 1414. Next

47. A meeting of the Senatus Academicus in Parliament Hall (renovated 1929-31). L. to r. the 'top table' officers are: Mr. R. Douglas (Senior Assistant Secretary); Mr. D.P. Dorward (Deputy Secretary); Dr. M.J.B. Lowe (Secretary and Registrar); Dr J. Steven Watson (Principal and Vice-Chancellor); Prof. M.A. Jeeves (Vice-Principal); and, Prof. D. Brynmor Thomas (Master of the United College).

day the Bulls were formally presented to Bishop Wardlaw in the refectory of the priory. Duly promulgated, the diocesan clergy and canons of the priory processed the Bulls into the cathedral church, singing a *Te Deum laudamus* . . . 'Thee, God, we praise . . .' Alexander Waghorn, Bishop of Ross, then intoned the versicle and collect of the Holy Ghost, *Deus qui corda fidelium.* There followed a High Mass at ten o'clock. A solemn procession was arranged for Tuesday, 6th February, the Feast of the Coming of St Andrew's Relics, and over four hundred clergy and novices walked around the town to celebrate the honour of the university's privileges. Prior James Bisset conducted the Mass and Bishop Waghorn preached.

Stage one of the founding of the university was to provide for a *studium generale* for preparing candidates in instruction in Theology, Canon Law (a digest of the formal decrees of councils, ecumenical, general, and local, of diocesan and natural synods, and of patriarchal decisions as to doctrine and discipline), Civil Law, Medicine and the Liberal Arts; and to present them for examination for license *ubique docendi* (which entitled them to teach anywhere in Christendom) to the Bishop. The first lecturers were unpaid (the only funds they had would be as priests) and they had to teach in private rooms in the town, or within the cloisters of the priory. Thereafter no man was allowed promotion or preferment without a university degree.

The head of the new university was the Rector. He was elected at the annual general congregation, or *Comitia,* of the university; the voting members of the *Comitia* were those who had matriculated. In his person the Rector embodied the dignity and corporate authority of the university. He presided over the general meetings, discipline and jurisdiction of the university and was assisted by assessors. The first Rector of the University was Laurence of Lindores (*circa.* 1373-1437), that inquisitor of heretics and propounder of Aristotelian physics. He it was, with Bishop Wardlaw, who was responsible for the burning of the first heretic in Scotland at St Andrews, one Paul Craw, martyred in Market Street in 1433.

Today the rôle of Rector has changed enormously and is stripped of its medieval powers, and derives its character from the Royal Commission of 1826, which resulted in the Act of 1858. The Rector is now President of the University Court and is elected by the matriculated students of the university and holds his office for three years. The first Rector after the new Act was Sir Ralph Anstruther, Bt., of Balcaskie, a local landowner. Down the decades international 'giants' have served as Rector, like the Norwegian explorer Fridtjof Nansen (served 1925-28) and the Italian inventor and engineer, Guglielmo, Marchese

49. A carnival charact[e] appearing in the 'Raisin Monday [ ] antics of the university's Martinm[ ]s Term.

Marconi (served 1934-37). In 1983 the students elected (her candidature was actually unopposed) the first woman Rector, the journalist Katherine Whitehorn.

The students have reason to rejoice if they have a 'working Rector' who can bring national influe[n]ce; but, in reality, the Rector can only effect student life through his or her personal patronage and inspirat[io]n. The student is affected by the *Senatus Academicus* rather than the University Court . . . the Rector ha[s] no say in the Senate.

The office of Chancellor was set up to generally supervise the whole of the university body, but, *e[x]tra mura.* The first man in this office, and described as *dominus cancellarius,* was Bishop Wardlaw, [a]nd, apart from four brief intervals (during the chancellorships of Lord Maitland, the Earl of Montrose, Ea[r] of Loudoun and Lord Menmuir), from 1413 to 1689, the office was held by a bishop or an archbis[ho]p. When Episcopacy was abolished, the appointment of the officer was assumed by the *Sen[at]us Academicus;* after the Act of 1858 the perogative was transferred to the General Council. [T]he Commissioners of 1826 noted this as a definition of the Chancellor's authority: 'The Chancellor is [t]he head of the University. He is consulted on all public matters relative to its welfare, and he is [al]so Conservator of its privileges. The power of conferring degrees is vested in him; this he may exercise ei[th]er personally when present, or by his depute when absent, with the advice of the doctors and masters of [t]he University. Nowadays the Chancellor is elected by the General Council and holds the office for life. [T]he present Chancellor is Sir Kenneth James Dover.

The 1858 Act empowers the Chancellor to appoint a Vice-Chancellor to discharge his office 'as rega[r]ds conferring degrees but in no other respect', although the office has been extant since the foundation of [t]he university. Since 1859 the Principal has been appointed Vice-Chancellor.

The office of the Principal of the University dates in effect from the Act of 1858, but was only crea[t]ed as such in 1953 when Sir Thomas Malcolm Knox was appointed. There were once two Principals [St Mary's and the United College) of whom the senior acted as University Principal. The Principal dire[c]ts the academic business of the university; his position has been under the patronage of the Crown and [h]e may serve until he is 70 years of age. The present Principal, Dr John Steven Watson was appointed [b]y the Crown on the advice of Ministers who in turn had taken soundings over the academic world. In fut[u]re a special University appointing committee will be set up. The retirement age, which was then fixed at [7]0 with Dr Watson's assent was followed by a controversial reduction of the retiring age for Professors fr[o]m 70 to 65. It was intended to mark a difference. Whether that will be continued depends upon action un[d]er the statutes.

The next major step in the development of the university was in 1419 when a gift of a tenement block by one Robert of Montrose 'chaplain of honour of the Apostolic See, secular canon of the Chapel Royal beside the monastery of St Andrews, and rector of the Church of Cults' was received. Set on the south side of South Street and located where the western part of Parliament Hall is now situated, this was dedicated to 'Almighty God, the Blessed Virgin Mary, and especially to the Blessed John the Evangelist and All Saints', to be used as a college of Theology and Art. In 1430 Bishop Wardlaw granted the adjoining tenement to St John's to serve as a school of Arts. These two institutions, the College of St John the Evangelist, and the *Paedagogium* were the precursors of the present College of St Mary (1537). The two establishments were confirmed by James I in 1432, who gave his blessing too to the university privileges. Charters followed to confirm, for instance, privileges granted by Archbishop Schevez in 1479, and the support of the Crown by James IV in 1512, James V in 1522, 1525, 1532 and 1535, James VI in 1579 and 1607, Charles I in 1633, Charles II in 1672 and James VII in 1685.

History now evolved so that a famous cleric could take up the centre stage of the university story. James Kennedy (*circa.* 1408-65) was a St Andrews graduate who became bishop of the diocese in 1440. Noted as 'the most distinguished Scotsman of his age' Kennedy had enormous influence and prestige in the life of the nation and church. His founding of a college was to be a seminal move in the development of the university.

The founding of the College of St Salvator on 27th August, 1450 by Bishop Kennedy was not only important for the university, but remains one of the most remarkable achievements of medieval Scotland. Kennedy endowed his college with his diocesan teinds (tithes) and his work was confirmed in 1451 by Pope Nicholas V, and again in 1458 a revised charter was granted by Pope Pius II. The bishop provided for the maintenance of 13 persons 'to recall the number of Our Lord and his twelve Apostles', and intended it for 'the teaching of theology and arts, for divine worship and scholastic exercise, and for the strengthening of the orthodox heretics.' Today the main frontage of Kennedy's college is virtually as it was in medieval times. The tower, to which the present spire was appended in 1550, still contains the original bells, although they have been re-cast. The entrance archway was formerly a part of the old cloister behind the church which still contains the Tournai style bomb of the founder. The building of the college, the chapel, the tomb and the bishop's great barge called the *St Salvator* cost the bishop the equivalent of £2.5

50. Charities 1982. Mackintosh Hall Float (the residence is commonly known as 'Chattan'), skippered by the Senior Student, Andrew Smith.

million in modern monies. St Salvator's chapel was renovated in the 18th century and in the 1920s. In the Spring of 1926 Bishop Kennedy's tomb was opened and the vault was found to be linked to the floor of the chapel by a small stair. When the air reached the burial area, after the vault door was opened, the bishop's coffin broke asunder, but Kennedy's remains were reinterred and so remain today.

As visitors stand before the great tower of St Salvator's they still wonder at the name, as no-one has heard of a 'St Salvator'! The key to the truth is that St Salvator's is a rendering of the old Scots *Sanct Salvatour* for Kennedy meant to dedicate his foundation to the Holy Saviour. At their feet, as the visitors gaze at the clock tower, are the initials 'P.H.' in the cobbles. We believe ourselves increasingly brutalised by the violence and cruelty that passes for entertainment on our television screens and in the cinemas. But who among the burghers of today could stand outside St Salvator's and watch a man burn to death and take six hours to do it, as did our Christian ancestors?

A Lutheran, Patrick Hamilton (*circa* 1504-28) came to St Andrews to compose music in the cathedral, but his studies of theology led him to be accused of heresy before Archbishop James Beaton. Hamilton went to Germany and returned in 1528 to openly attack the established church in Scotland. He was arrested and condemned to death for heresy. On the 29th February, 1528 he was burned before the gates of St Salvator's. One legend which grew up out of his martyrdom was that the psychic power of his death etched his face into the stonework above the tower gateway and that it is visible today on the North Street side of the tower.

St Leonard's College was founded 20th August, 1512 by Archbishop Alexander Stewart (1495-1513) in conjunction with Prior John Hepburn of the Augustinian Priory of Canons Regular of the town. Stewart was the bastard son of James IV and was called 'a pupil most promising, versatile and accomplished' by his tutor, the Dutch Renaissance humanist Desiderius Erasmus (1466-1536). The young archbishop, however, fell at Flodden and was able to do no more than co-found the college as one for 'Poor Clerks of St Andrews' (that is Clerks in Holy Orders, and novices). The college was never given Papal confirmation, but the Cardinal Archbishop David Beaton gave it a charter in 1545 in his capacity as Apostolic Legate. For the new college an old *hospitium,* and the church of St Leonard beside it were allocated; the *hospitium* had been used as an almshouse for aged women, but as the cathedral authorities considered the women of 'little fruit either of devoutness and virtue', they were evicted. The church was re-roofed in 1910 and re-furbished 1948-52 and belongs to the university. The other buildings and site belonging to the college are now in the ownership of St Leonards School.

The rules of the college are interesting to contemplate in terms of modern academic informality. For instance each hour of the day had its devotional or educational duty. Speech was to be in Latin only and students were expected to take on domestic duties. No women were allowed within the college except for a laundress who had to be fifty years of age at least and, by inference, plain. Students could not move outside the college without special permission and were forbidden to play 'dishonest games' like football! The *regents,* or teaching staff, were responsible for discipline within the college. A relic of the regent system survived into the 1960s when teaching staff would have 'at homes' for students. The practice has

51. Installation of Sir James Barrie as Rector, 3rd May, 1922. L. to r.: Dr. James Younger of Mount Melville, the Chancellor's Assessor; Sir James Irvine, Principal and Vice-Chancellor (1921-52); Sir James Matthew Barrie, and, Field-Marshal the Earl Haig of Bemersyde, Rector 1916-19.

52. Robert John Graham Boothby, 1st Baron Boothby was Rector 1958-61; the name of his 'float' parodies a popular television programme of the day and the name of the Principal, Sir Malcolm Knox. The student reading is George Taylor.

53. Frank Muir samples delicacies with Oliver Ash, President of the S.R.C. at the special dinner to celebrate Muir's last presiding over the General Council as Rector. The famous writer and broadcaster was Rector 1976-79.

54. The university's first woman Rector, Katharine Whitehorn, is 'dragged' past the 14th century Pends gateway, on her first tour of the town.

55. Baker Lane (right) is a fine example of an old St Andrews 'close'. Abutting the lane is part of the Dept. of Medieval History of the university and next to it through a pend, with a fine iron gate, is the property known as St John's (67-69 South Street), perhaps the oldest house standing in St Andrews. The medieval building, now housing a centre for Advanced Historical Studies, owes its name to its former owners, the Order of Knights of the Hospital of St John of Jerusalem. They were a partly monastic, partly military order pledged to assist the crusading kingdom of Jerusalem against the infidels, to tend the sick and guard the pilgrim routes to the Holy Land. Once the knights were major property holders in the town, but it is unlikely that knights of the order ever resided here, in reality they were only drawing rents. Once, the properties were owned by Patrick Adamson, Archbishop of St Andrews (1575-92), who made them his principal residence, the palace-castle being no longer habitable. The property was renovated by the university in 1974.

now died out with the coming of the 'academic families' wherein students have fellow-student 'mothers' and 'fathers' to guide them in the wrinkles of student life. Nevertheless modern students entering a Faculty have a Tutor (Arts) and an Advisor of Studies (Science), or Regent (Theology) to whom they can turn for academic advice, or assistance in other matters. On Raisin Monday, during Martinmas term, the *bejants* and *bejantines* present to their 'academic parents' a traditional pound of raisins (today in the form of a bottle of wine) in exchange for a ribald receipt in Latin . . . the occasion is celebrated in carnival costumes.

The *Paedagogium*—the first 'school' associated with the university was erected into a separate college and endowed with the teinds of the church of St Michael of Tarvit, near Cupar. Archbishop James Beaton petitioned the Pope for confirmation which came in a Bull in 1537 from Paul III; thereafter it was denominated St Mary's. The new college was completed by Archbishop John Hamilton in 1550 and confirmed in its final form by Pope Julius III in 1552. Basically the college was organised as a seminary for the training of secular priests in Arts, Theology and Canon Law. This college exists today and Divinity is taught in the pleasant 16th century buildings with their own quadrangle abutting the old university library, now converted for the department of Psychology.

Thus was the university formed at the coming of the Reformation in 1560. Following the 'New Foundation of the University and Colleges of St Andrews' the colleges of St Salvator and St Leonard were confirmed to the subjects of Philosophy, Law and Medicine while (Reformed) Theology was exclusive to St Mary's. This system remained until the 'great reform' of 1858.

Throughout the 16th century almost all of the leading figures in church and state in Scotland were educated in St Andrews. At the Reformation the university was stripped of its 'popish' influence, but the university did become the nub of a new national scheme of education grounded in the parish schools

University life was regularly interrupted by the political troubles of the 16th and 17th centuries, but it retained its academic influence, eminence and importance in the education system in Scotland. Following the Act of Union in 1707, and the abolition of Episcopacy in the established church previous to the Act, St Andrews, with its port and university, declined. The need for economies pressured the two colleges of St Salvator and St Leonard to amalgamate as the single United College in 1747, and the collegiate residency was also gradually abandoned.

The university survived throughout the 18th century and achieved a slow recovery in the 19th century when St Andrews itself underwent a commerical revival. During 1826-30 the university was subject to a searching investigation by Royal Commission. This provided it with much required new buildings and changes in the constitution and courses of study were revised. These were underlined by parliamentary sanction in 1858. As the century developed, Principals like Brewster, Tulloch and Forbes, headed an academic staff of outstanding distinction. From 1886 to 1915 the university expanded rapidly and although it maintained its reputation for Theology, Classics and Philosophy, Science was established as an important academic discipline. University buildings developed—thanks to such benefactors as Andrew Carnegie, the Scottish-American philanthropist, who served as Rector of the University from 1901-07— and collegiate residence was once more revived. Prominent university buildings of medieval date remain but the majority these days show the architectural fashions of 1870-1970.

The affiliation of the University College of Dundee in 1881 to 'make it form part of the University of St Andrews' was effected in 1897 and in 1898 the Conjoint School of Medicine was established at Dundee. The foundation of the University of Dundee in 1967 brought all the arrangements to an end and consequently St Andrews lost its accomplishment in Medicine and Law. Today the university, with its three Faculties of Arts, Divinity and Science, is still in the forefront of higher education. St Leonard's college was recently revived as a non-statutory college to care for postgraduate students, and to encourage research activities.

Today the university only offers a pre-clinical course in medicine, within the Faculty of Sciences, leading to a Bachelor of Science (Medical Science); nevertheless by formal agreement students receive further training towards graduation in Medicine at Manchester University. Yet, both town and gown have contributed down the years in both academic medicine and general practice. Two men may be remembered as contributing positively to both, James Orr and Sir James Mackenzie.

'He was an ideal family doctor, and his cheery and kindly disposition made his presence a real tonic to his patients . . .': thus was James Orr described at the time of his death. Born in 1876 at Hawick, the son of the Rev. Dr James Orr, Professor of Apologetics at Edinburgh and Glasgow Universities, James Orr Jr., was educated at George Watson's and the University of Edinburgh. He graduated M.B., Ch.B., (1899) . . . M.R.C.P. (1927) . . . and came to St Andrews in 1900. Orr had been the Resident Medical Officer of a City Poorhouse, Craiglockhart, Edinburgh, and House Surgeon at the Royal Infirmary, Dundee. In St Andrews he became a partner in the general practice of Orr & Macleod. He is remembered academically for his work as Clinician at the James Mackenzie Institute in The Scores (the actual building today is the annexe of the Scores Hotel). Founded in 1919 by Sir James Mackenzie (1853-1925), the Institute and its work was way ahead of its time. Sir James was a prominent heart specialist and pioneered investigative clinical procedures towards a basis of preventative medicine. With the help of local GPs, Sir James held regular meetings at The Scores clinic and established a thorough set of medical records of St Andrews people. This work was carried on in the 1940s when its research endowment passed to the Faculty of Medicine (and allied academic disciplines) and the Child Care Centre at Dyersbrae. James Orr died in 1944.

The position of the students has changed enormously in five hundred years. In the early days students could be as young as 13. One such student was James Crichton of Eliock (1560-83) who matriculated at St Andrews at the age of ten, graduating four years later. A distinguished scholar and soldier, Crichton, bynamed 'The Admirable', is said to have lived in the turretted house at the end of Butts Wynd, North Street.

56. Madras College, Kilrymont Road, officially opened 1968.

Until the modern education acts the student intake showed that the gentry predominated. The sons of craftsmen and tenant farmers were not uncommon, but the sons of artisans and labourers are difficult to identify and had a dilemma in obtaining a patron. While the student often found it novel to rank as a venerable doctor in general university elections, his position as freshman (the term *bejant* for such dates from the late 18th century, with *bejantine* for females) was one of underdog to senior students. One year of being a *bejant* led to life as a *semi,* in third year a *tertian,* and as a *magistrand* in final year.

These days student vocabulary is less indivdualistic and colourful than in the past, oaths not counted! In the past a definite 'student-speak' was identifiable. For instance a *waster,* was a student who was idle, or profligate; a *grinder* was a hard worker. A *bunk* was the private lodging of a student, and a *spree* an entertainment (rowdy or not). A *solatium* was a spree organised by the Debating Society (held in December or January) and a *gaudeamus* was a festival towards the end of a session. To *plough, pluck* or *spin* was to fail one's examinations. The *comp* was an examination for entrance scholarships, and the *cage* was the glass notice-box in which examination results lists were posted. Today an example of modern studentese would be *ya*—an 'upper-class' (even if it is in their own minds) student whose 'uniform' is a pair of green wellington boots, a sleeveless waistcoat worn over a jumper or shirt, and a flat cap. This is also the outdoor dress of the *Sloane* (from 'Sloane Street Ranger' of London, of which the Chief Ranger is the Princess of Wales).

In earlier days most students lived in the town in *bunks* with a landlady of varying ferocity; today most students live in residence. Men's Residences are St Salvators Hall (1930) and Hepburn Hall (1947), females reside in University Hall (1896), and 'mixed' residences are found at McIntosh Hall (1930), Andrew Melville Hall (1968), David Russell Hall (1971), Deanscourt (1951), Hamilton Hall (1949), John Burnet Hall (1965) and St Regulus Hall (1944). Because of their residency a gulf may be expanding between the modern student and the townsfolk whom he considers as 'parochial'.

Writing in 1911 about student life, the late C.Hilton Brown wrote thus of *bunks* . . . 'The St Andrews bunk is any one's who finds the door unbarred; he neither knocks nor rings, nor considers the suitability of the hour. It is understood that his host will be glad to see him; if not, he will say so. One borrows amazingly, and about this community of property there is something very charming. If one's cupboard is empty, one sallies forth in search of one that is full, and it is no unusual thing to find on one's table a note which says 'Have borrowed your hat to go home.'' '

57. Kate Kennedy (played by Nick Brown), her 'uncle' Bishop James Kennedy (Peter Fitzsimmons, President of the Kate Kennedy Club), and page (B. Collins), emerge from 'The Master's House', during Kate Kennedy 1983. On the steps stand Professor D. Brynmor Thomas (Master of the United College) and Mrs Thomas.

58. Archbishop James Sharp (1618-79), a character in the Kate Kennedy pageant, played here by Lewis Derrick. Sharp changed his ecclesiastical coat from Presbyterian to Scottish Episcopacy and became Archbishop of St Andrews and *ex officio* Chancellor of the university in 1661. A devoted persecutor of the Covenanters (the name given to signatories of the Scottish National Covenant in 1638 who were pledged to uphold the Presbyterian faith against prelacy and popery), Sharp was murdered by David Hackston of Rathillet and a group of fanatical Calvinists as his coach, on its way from Edinburgh to St Andrews, crossed nearby Magus Muir. Sharp was butchered in the sight of his daughter Isabel. Today his tomb is still to be seen in Holy Trinity Church and there is a monument commemorating the murder to be seen on Magus Muir.

59. H.M. Queen Elizabeth II shakes hands with the university Chancellor, Sir Kenneth James Dover, during the royal visit to the town in 1982. Directly behind the Queen stands Brevet-Colonel Sir John Gilmour, Bt, of Montrave, H.M. Lord Lieutenant of Fife, and H.R.H. The Prince Philip.

The town's attitudes to students have mellowed, for as grants have increased (plus parental subsidies), the students bring much coin to tinkle in the tills of the town. Yet eyebrows have often been raised at student antics, as C. Hilton Brown again wrote in 1911: 'The old strifes of town and gown are now hushed except during the Parliamentary elections, when I have seen great things done outside Henderson's shop in Church Street, but there remains among certain sections of the community a lingering and incredible terror of the student and his ways. I recall one of my earliest experiences of St Andrews as walking along South Street in the dusk and hearing a tremendous uproar of singing approaching from the Cathedral end. I passed two worthy ladies in conversation, and one of them said "IT'S THE STUDENTS." She said it so,—in large capitals; she spoke as though it were a manifestation of the Hosts of Darkness; she was genuinely apprehensive.' These days the St Andreans are no longer surprised by student activities.

The Students' Union is a very young appendage to university life. By 1864 a reading room for students had been established in the cloister behind St Salvator's College chapel, and there was some attention to providing sports facilities. Early in 1885 a Students' Representative Council was formed which gave its attention to the forming of a Union, and such was opened in temporary premises in 1888. In 1892 it moved to permanent quarters at the corner of Butts Wynd. A new Union was opened in the 1970s in St Mary's Place on the site of the old West Park Hotel. Run by a Management Committee the Union provides cheap food and drink and other facilities for students. The Management Committee helps fund the student newspaper *Aien*. Today the Students' Representative Council (S.R.C.) makes representation to the university authorities on all matters concerning students. The President of the S.R.C. is a member of the University Court and Senate; three students representatives are also elected members of the Senate. Some hundred or so student societies are affiliated to the S.R.C., ranging from a Gilbert and Sullivan Society to a Chess Club.

61. A corner of the 'big room' of the R & A showing the members' lockers. Above (l. to r.) are pictures of the Captain (the Rt. Hon. A.J. Balfour) driving off on Medal Day at St Andrews, 1894; H.R.H. Edward, Prince of Wales (captain, 1922) by Sir William Orpen, 1925; and, John Whyte Melville of Mount Melville, by Sir Francis Grant, 1873.

60. *(facing page)* The medieval Swilken Bridge leads to a famous view of the Old Course.

62. Crails Lane runs between Market St and South St and was well-developed as a 'close' (Scottish for a narrow alley) by the 1500s. There is evidence that the properties on the left were once single-storey dwellings and the building on the right dates from 1724 (renovated 1950). Although much changed, Crails Lane retains its character and mid-way along, and looking north, there is an unexpected view of St Salvator's Tower. 'Pepita's Restaurant' was first opened in 1974 as a vegetarian and wholefood eating house by Ms. Pepita Quinn; it was taken over by Mr. Michael Henretty in 1977 and is now a coffee shop and bistro.

In the late Spring, the Kate Kennedy Club members gird their loins for their annual carnival. This colourful costume pageant seems to have originated in 1849 as an end-of-term 'rag' by the final-year Arts students of the university It takes its name from the following circumstances. The old bell in the tower of the Collegiate Church of St Salvator has been long known as 'Katherine'—supposedly named after the college founder's, Bishop Kennedy, legendary niece Kate. At the 'rag' one student is thought to have dressed up as 'Kate' and capered at the centre of the noisy masquerade. The 'rag' was successful and was repeated until within a short time it became a tradition. As the professors attempted to suppress it, the tradition became a symbol of undergraduate freedom.

By the 1860s the pageant had spilled out from the university precincts and became an elaborate procession through the streets. Each year student high spirits led to confrontation with the local authorities and the Kate Kennedy Procession was suppressed in 1874; a ban which was virtually total until 1926.

Today it has become a vibrant costume pageant with some sixty to seventy characters taking part. The *dramatis personae,* played by members of the Kate Kennedy Club, are all connected with St Andrews and its university in some way, from St Andrew himself to Field-Marshal the Earl Haig of Bemersyde (a former Rector). Traditionally Kate Kennedy is played by a male student, and 'she' rides in a carriage with her uncle who is dressed in full canonicals.

The procession emerges from the university Quad and winds down North Street to the Castle, via The Scores. Then, by way of Market Street, the West Port and the cathedral, it returns to the Quad.

Possibly the procession might have had an inspiration older than the 19th century. Kate's name could be a version of *Cath Cinneachaidh,* the Gaelic for the 'Rebirth of Spring'. Indeed, in 1432 the university authorities condemned a new pagan Spring rite practiced by the students as 'Useless, unprofitable, dangerous and damnable.'

The pageant is organised by the Kate Kennedy Club which was founded in 1926 by Donald Kennedy and James Doak. These two were inspired by the rectorial address on 'Courage' by Sir James Matthew Barrie (1860-1937), who was Rector in 1919. In that address Barrie had mused on the supposition as to which historical figures associated with the university he would have liked to have met personally. Kennedy and Doak saw the revival of a procession of such characters as the nearest one could get to Barrie's idea. They persuaded the then Principal, Sir James Irvine, to lift the 19th century ban, on the assurance that former satirising and insulting of the town and gown personalities would not be repeated. Today the stated aims of the Kate Kennedy Club, which remains an all-male organisation, are to 'preserve traditions, to raise money for charity and to foster town-gown relationships.'

Principals have come and gone, but one who left his mark was Sir James Colquhoun Irvine (1877-1952). A strict disciplinarian, Sir James, known to generations of students as 'Jimmy the Princ', re-introduced the collegiate system and was a tireless collector of monies with which to expand the university. Indeed, following his commencement as Principal in 1922, the university began its biggest expansion since the original foundation of the medieval colleges. A notable chemist, Sir James did sterling service to the country in research work during World War II, and to mark 25 years of his principalship, students past and contemporary endowed the Irvine Medal in Chemistry. In his tribute to him at a memorial service, the Very Rev. Charles L. Warr, Dean of the Thistle, had this to say of Sir James who was deemed to personify the 'St Andrews man' and to imbue the 'spirit of the university': 'He was in the classical tradition of these great Scotsmen who owed nothing to rank and fortune but everything to their own dynamic character and natural abilities. Only Scotland could have moulded him to what he was. Indeed, to the eager lad at the Technical College of Glasgow sixty years ago, perhaps only Scotland could have afforded the opportunity of becoming all that he subsequently became. One would have liked to have known James Irvine in his youth; to have watched the earliest flash of his genius, and the first adventurings of that questing mind which probed and searched down every path of life and thought and never rested till the hour of death. Part of the secret of his life's achievement was that he lived and laboured unencumbered by many of the self-made complications which clutter up the mind of lesser men. He was utterly devoid of vanity, and he had no personal ambitions. The honours which were showered upon him gave him a single pleasure. They were unsought, and he bore them very lightly.

'It was characteristic of his generous heart that the honours that interested him most were those that came to his friends. His was in fact, a dedicated life. He was concerned only with placing his gifts and abilities at the service of his day and generation. He sought no reward for any work he did, but, to whatever he put his hand, he brought an inflexible purpose and a determination to brook nothing that in his view might hinder its eventual success. He would fight to the last for his convictions, whether with others, or alone. A mind as clear, and a personality so strong and forceful, inevitably at times

encountered, and even invited, criticism; but we can confidently leave him and his life and work to the judgement of posterity.'

Writing in her husband's biography *The Avenue of Years* (Blackwood, 1970) the late Mabel Irvine (d.1967) wrote of 'the St Andrews spirit': 'But the spirit of St Andrews was a real thing and a good thing. It bound together the small band of students who realised that if their numbers were few, the knowledge they were seeking had no boundaries. They wrote poetry about it and it is a good thing to write poetry in one's youth, so long as the conviction follows that it is not very good poetry. They sang about it, they were called the Singing University in those days, and the songs from the Scarlet Gown set to music by John Farmer were better worth singing than the cheap music hall ditties they have sung of late years. They were proud of their red gowns, and about the grey streets, or clustered in the deep embrasure of the Castle windows against the blue sea, or in a long line of scarlet down the pier on Sunday morning after chapel service, or filling the chapel with a shaft of sunlight athwart them, the scarlet gown always looked magnificent.'

The red gown goes from 'in' to 'out' and back again in fashion, from the throngs of chapel-goers who still wear it, to the student who preferred his Worker's Revolutionary Party badge to a gown (albeit of his political colours)—'We came here to study not to wear a bloody red gown.'

Coming to the university enclave in 1905 Mable Irvine had this to say about social life: 'That early life in St Andrews had an atmosphere which I find hard to define; calm, cultured, leisured and secure; both town and University contained a small circle and, in the large houses in the surrounding county, an unusual number of distinguished and interesting people. Sunday tea was a happy institution. The silver urn hissed on the tea table above Rockingham china, hot buttered scones, shortbread and gingerbread. The fire blazed and the winter afternoon was shut out by drawn curtains. Young lecturer and elderly professors met on terms of easy intimacy and friendly argument.'

It was the custom for lecturers to hold 'open house' on a Sunday morning, and most 'teas' included musical entertainment. Indeed 'musical evenings' at which junior and senior lecturers met were popular and dinner parties were still very formal. Evening dress was worn and junior lecturer guests were not

64.   Newspaper delivery boys and girls of 'Good News'. Back Row: Alastair Smith; Andrew Watt; Colin Brown; Peter Finnigan; June Elder. Middle Row: Jennifer Williamson; Gavin Irvine; Douglas Palompo; Alan Smith. Front Row: Richard Harris; William Bews; Mark Small; Jack Brown.

63.   *(facing page)* Blackfriars from the roof of Madras College; the tree in the foreground is a Wild Cherry, or 'Gean'.

65. Since 1976 the 'Four Woods' restaurant at 117 North St has been personally supervised by Elma and David Moffat.

expected to leave before any professor, or senior lecturer present. Mable Irvine remembered one tradition: 'The old-fashioned custom that for six months a bride took precedence of every other guest no matter what her rank, was firmly adhered to. For this reason it was considered a compliment to one's hostess to wear one's wedding-gown. "That wedding-dress of yours," Jim used to complain, "has cost me a fortune in cabs", because in a more manageable dress we liked to walk arm-in-arm to our parties on a fine night, and in so doing we were rewarded by many a beautiful sight. The moon shining high above the broken piers of the Cathedral, or behind the College Tower, or from our own doorstep, making a path across the burnished steel of the Bay. Why miss it all by jogging along in a musty old one-horse cab?'

Dinners, of course, lasted for hours and often ran to six courses. Inflation, and the need for lecturers to work harder to afford the luxuries (or basic essentials, depending how you look at them) have tended to kill off the lavish home entertaining of the past.

If poetry reigns no more, art certainly does, with both town and gown contributing to painting and sculpture. The St Andrews Art Club holds regular exhibitions and the Crawford Centre for the Arts, opened in 1978, and situated in North Street and by the department of Art History, contains the Balcarres Gallery and a drama studio.

The university is still undoubtedly the main employer in the town, with the small 'industrial estate' to the south of the town providing work for a few. Tourism and its allied spin-offs brought by the golf-links also brings a regular pool of employment.

Probably the first association of guildsmen in St Andrews was the Guild of Cathedral Builders, who regulated the quality of the work in the town, supervised the apprentices and monitored the welfare of the brother stonemasons. To follow a trade in medieval St Andrews one had to be a freeman, who was supposed to live within the city boundaries; these men were also expected to defend the city with military service. The privileges of freemanship included having prime sites at the weekly markets and seasonal fairs. Each of the trades and crafts had its own guild with its special badges and livery. Besides the self-regulation of the trade in the burgh, the town council elected a warden who protected the inhabitants from shoddy goods and exorbitant prices. The separate guilds were controlled by a deacon, and the senior guildsmen formed a council of management which had as one of its main tasks the maintenance of the patronage of their individual altars in the Parish Church of the Holy Trinity. Set now in South Street, between Logie's Lane and Church Street (formerly called The Vennel) the 'Town Kirk' was once located behind the east gable of the cathedral and dated from the 12th century. In 1140 Sir William Lindsy of the Byres gave 'six rigges' of land in South Street for a new parish church, and in this church, up to the

66. David Joy, illustrator and glass engraver, of The Grange, works on a glass engraving commemorating town photographer, George Middlemas Cowie (1902-82). Cowie gave the University of St Andrews over 60,000 negatives, on his retirement, which form a unique photographic record of local and country life.

67. Bill Bishop carries on the tradition of wheel building in the premises of Gordon Christie which were taken over by Leslie Dickson in 1965.

Reformation, the guildsmen had their altars. Among the most beautiful of the guild altars were those of St Aubert, the canonised Bishop of Cambrai, who was the patron of the Baker's Guild, and St Bartholomew, Apostle and martyr, the patron of the butchers and the leatherworkers. The guildsmen would have right of burial in the churchyard of Holy Trinity, which once extended to the centre of the present-day South Street and filled Church Square. Today specialised craftsmen still exist, but as individuals and not within a guild brotherhood, and pursue their trade in such crafts as glass engraving, pottery and woodworking.

The guilds also did much work in protecting families who fell on hard times and subsidised widows and orphans, and pioneered an education in the basic accomplishments of reading and writing for boys as well as girls.

The changing face of attitudes towards women has been clearly seen in St Andrews. The Married Women's Property Act of 1882, extended in 1893, kicked open the door for more women to be treated as individuals with social rights. Yet these things were only helping the women of financial substance. In 1905 representatives of the Women's Social and Political Union (the 'Suffragettes') speaking at Cupar underlined the plight of poor women as drudges in a man's world: 'For fifty years she had made artificial flowers . . .' said one speaker about a sweat-shop worker. 'She can neither read nor write. Her rates of pay are, for making violets 7d. a gross, geraniums 7d. a gross, buttercups 3d. a gross, roses 1s.3d. to 3s.6d. a gross. Her average working day is 14 hours and her average earnings 10s. weekly. Her husband is also a flower-maker, but is nearly blind and quite an invalid. Until recently they occupied an underground room, for which 4s.6d. weekly was paid.' So the 'Sweated Industries' flourished even in St Andrews with such a wage quoted in modern currency as 50p per week, some £4 in today's *pro-rata* prices of which more than 50 percent was for accommodation. Locally women's anger was fermented, as the Suffragettes set fire to Leuchars station!

Revolutionary changes were seen in St Andrews in the education of women. In medieval times no woman was allowed to set foot within the colleges of St Andrews. Indeed in 1574 the 4th Earl of Morton had insisted that 'the wives and bairds' of lecturers should not be allowed to live in college property.

Despite the collapse of the possibilities of higher education for women which had been served by the nunneries swept away at the Reformation, some basic education for women in Scotland did exist as witnessed by the Statutes of Icolmkill (*videlicet:* Iona) passed by James VI in 1609. It is probable therefore that some primary education for girls in the burgh schools of St Andrews was available before 1700.

In the first half of the 19th century, girls in any middle-class family were usually kept at home to be tutored by governesses, and certainly university education for women hardly existed in any form before Queen's College, London, was opened in 1848. Nevertheless, St Andrews was in the forefront of the development of higher education of women in Scotland by the institution of the L.L.A. scheme in 1877. The project was designed to entitle women to enter for examinations held in the UK (and, later abroad) and successful candidates were granted the title 'Literate in Arts'. After 1881 the title was expanded to 'Lady Literate in Arts' (L.L.A.) and the scheme continued until 1932.

The leading light in the project for women was William Knight, Professor of Moral Philosophy (1876-1903). He too promoted a bursary fund for women students and helped raise a fund to build and equip a Hall of Residence. Women students did not make their appearance within the colleges until 1892, and it was not until 'The University Hall of Residence for Women Students' was opened in 1896 that women lived on campus. In 1904 a Women's Union was established through the endowment of Mrs Andrew Carnegie.

St Andrews was to see the first woman to take a degree of Bachelor of Divinity. Miss Frances Melville, while Warden of University Hall, attended courses at St Mary's College and graduated in 1910. The first female lecturer within the university was Miss Alice Marion Umpherston, Lecturer in Philosophy 1896-98. By 1911 there were 251 women students at the university and there are today 1,690 female undergraduates representing 53.3 percent of the total undergraduate community 1983-84.

A further step forward in women's education was achieved with the establishment of St Leonards School. The first Headmistress was (Dame) Louisa Lumsden (1840-1935) who had been educated abroad and at Girton College, Cambridge, and had been a classics' mistress at Cheltenham Ladies College. The

68. Jurek Alexander Putter works on one of his authoritative and academic pictorial reconstructions of St Andrews at his studio at Burgers Close, 141 South Street.

69. The Lade Braes is a popular St Andrews walk all the year round. The Kinness Burn follows its own narrow valley into the south side of the town, and once it supplied the power for the old Law Mill hereabouts.

school was opened on the 2 October, 1877 on a site at the foot of Queen's Gardens now occupied by the mixed residence of St Regulus Hall, and adjoining the gardens of St Mary's College. Incidentally Louisa Lumsden became Warden of University Hall in 1895, and the extension to University Hall in modern times was named after her.

The real founders of St Leonards were members of the Ladies' Educational Association, particularly Mrs Matthew Rodger, wife of the minister of St Leonard's Parish Church, and Mrs Lewis Campbell, the wife of the Professor of Greek at the university. A company was formed to administer the school and articles of Association were subscribed. The school's first Council chairman was John Tulloch, Principal of St Mary's College from 1854-1886.

For the outset the curriculum was liberal and wide, spanning tuition from Latin to Mathematics, and from Greek to Science and Modern Languages. The school pioneered gymnastic lessons (physical training did not appear until 1895 in the Scottish Day School Code) and sent its first student to Cambridge in 1880. In 1881 the Council bought a house in the grounds of what had been St Leonard's College and the school re-opened in 1882, changing its name from St Andrews School for Girls to St Leonards. On its new site the school began with a group of three buildings; today it includes thirty acres of parkland for extensive playing fields, school houses, classrooms, laboratories and a gymnasium. In modern times St Leonards has been acknowledged as one of the leading schools for girls in the United Kingdom. It is governed by a Council whose members are drawn from all over the country, representing both academic and business life.

St Leonards School library is housed in a building of great interest and uniqueness. The edifice is 16th century and once belonged to the Chamberlain of James Stewart, Earl of Moray, half-brother of Mary, Queen of Scots. It was begun in 1523 by Hew Scrymgeour, a local merchant, and received its name from Mary's visit of 1564, when she is supposed to have occupied rooms on the top floor of the west wing. Mary is said to have practiced archery in the garden. The house's later extension is called Priorsgate.

70. The Quad of the Madras College; the south side of the Quad was ready and opened for the first pupils on 1st October 1833. In 1843 the Quad was paved with Caithness slabs.

The numbers of girls at St Leonards rose steadily and it was decided to open a preparatory department. So a junior school, called St Katherines, was opened in 1894 in the Adam detail house in North Street, built *circa* 1812 by R.Barbour. Today that house is a part of the university department of Art History.

A 'first' linking women, town and education arises from the early St Katherines, for the second mistress from the foundation was Miss Frances J. Warrack M.B.E., who became St Andrews' first woman Town Councillor in 1919. When in 1975 St Andrews became a part of North East Fife District for local government purposes only a few women still showed any interest in local government service, and today out of a District Council of eighteen only three are women.

Another school which has played a prominent part in the development of education in St Andrews, is The Madras College. Madras takes its name from a system of education invented by Rev. Dr. Andrew Bell (1753-1832), Prebendary of Westminster Abbey and Master of Sherburn Hospital. A native of St Andrews and a graduate of the university, Bell, after tutoring for a short while in American, returned to the burgh and by 1784 he determined to become an Anglican clergyman.

Deciding on India as his next piece of wanderlust, Bell was appointed a chaplain to the Honourable East India Company and became involved in education in 1789 in the Male Military Orphan Asylum of Madras. Here he devised a monitor system (senior boys taught the younger ones, and were themselves supervised by masters), which was ultimately to be used throughout the United Kingdom and the West Indies. While in India, Bell amassed a fortune and returned to Britain and became Rector of Swanage in 1801 and established himself as a landowner.

Bell now turned his eye to his hometown of St Andrews, although he was an infrequent visitor. He first bought land to the south side of the ruinous chapel of the Black Friars in South Street. Here was to be developed his new school; alas he died weeks before his idea came to fruition. The first part of the building was far enough advanced at the south side of the quad to receive the first pupils on 1st October, 1833. In 1963 the old Burgh School (1890) was fused with Madras as a part of the 'comprehensivisation' programme. The new Kilrymont buildings were occupied by Madras pupils in 1967 and officially opened in 1968. It is said that until the turn of the 19th century the reputation of the teaching at Madras was enough to bring families to live in St Andrews.

Before Madras was built there were two main public schools with approximately nine private schools. In those days anyone could start a school without any qualifications. The two public schools were the English School (*circa.* 1750), to the northwest of Holy Trinity, where the public library is now, and the Grammar School (a 17th century foundation with Latin as the main subject taught), lying between Blackfriars and the Lade Braes Lane. Apart from Madras and St Leonards, the town is served by Canongate Primary school, Langlands, Lawhead Primary, St Andrews Nursery, and Greyfriars.

Blackfriars is still closely associated with the Madras buildings designed by the architect William Burn of Edinburgh in the Jacobean style. All that remains today is the chapel of the north transept (1525) of the original church founded in the 15th century for the Order of Dominican Friars (the Black Friars) and dedicated to the Assumption and Coronation of the Blessed Virgin Mary. Blackfriars suffered as a consequence of the infamous sermon of John Knox on 14th June, 1559; it was granted as a property to the municipality of St Andrews by Mary, Queen of Scots in 1567. It is said that the Black Friars were brought to Scotland by William de Malvoisine (d.1238), Bishop of St Andrews, in the 13th century. Somewhere in the church was buried the cadaver of the Cardinal Archbishop David Beaton. It is interesting to note, before the Reformation, university meetings were regularly held within the monastery of the Black Friars and one Dean of the Faculty of Theology was John Grierson, Provincial of the Order.

A piece of architecture which also takes the tourists' eye, and irritates the nerves as he or she waits in the line of traffic, is the West Port. The gateway as it is seen today was reconstructed in 1589 by the mason John Robertson of Blebo, on the model of the Netherbow Port at Edinburgh which was demolished in 1764. The West Port, which was very old at its reconstruction, was renovated in 1843, when huge buttresses, which projected into the street, were removed and the more elegant buttresses substituted; at this time the side arches were inserted.

An unchanging walk, except by seasons, in St Andrews is the Lade Braes, which reaches into the heart of the burgh. Running down the east side of Madras grounds is Lade Braes Lane linking the eastern section of the Lade Braes walkway, above the Kinness Burn, with Queen's Terrace. Across Bridge Street is the western section of the Lade Brae's Walk leading through Cockshaugh Park to Law Mill (1750).

Those golfers who enter St Andrews by, say, the courtesy car from the Old Course and Country Club, or come across the links while walking down The Scores, will be forgiven for initial disappointment. The immediate reaction is one of shock. Could this place of gorse, dunes and sandpits be *the* hallowed ground? Indeed,

71. Herein light and dark play tricks on the eye, so that as one stares at this picture of a window of the north transept of Blackfriars, the figure of a cowled friar slowly emerges.

72. Filming a sequence of 'Chariots of Fire' along the West Sands.

the famed Old Course is not a set of beautiful manicured layouts, so fashionable these days, backed by cosseted flowering shrubs and nurtured trees; yet, it is golf's premier play area presenting one of the toughest golf tests in the world within the most atmospheric of all sports scenes.

Games of club and ball are common to most countries but the game as we know it today owes its origins to Scotland, and St Andrews is the 'Mecca for Golfers' bar none. The earliest historical reference to golf in Scotland is found in the year 1457, when James II, King of Scots, forbade the playing of golf (and football) as it kept men away from their archery practice. The local Kirk Sessions were much against golf too, particularly in the 16th century, as it encouraged players to profane the sabbath, and the very officers of the Kirk were neglectful of their duties because of the game.

Undoubtedly the earliest note of golf in St Andrews is dated 1552, but the game was played elsewhere in Scotland as early as 1413. Although the game was generally indulged in most actively by the gentry, golf on the Old Course was free of charge to all comers, inhabitants and visitors until 1913. then a fee was made for visitors. From 1912 to 1945 St Andrews ratepayers could play free, but in 1946 an annual subscription was imposed. Today the maintenance of the courses is in the hands of the Links Management Committee.

In 1921 Bobby Jones (1902-71) first competed at the Old Course and considered it 'the worst course on earth'. He left in disgust, but later averred that it was 'the very best'. Scottish ace, Eric Brown, cursed the Old Course as 'a dirt track', and Jack Nicklaus referred to it as 'cattle pasture' in 1964. But, by his win at the British Open in 1970 he had become more reverential with the comment, 'If a golfer is to be remembered he must win at St Andrews.' Of all the courses the 72-par Old Course, with its first fairway 367 yards wide dwarfs in honour the nearby New (opened 1895), the Jubilee (1897) and the Eden (1914). Some would say that the Old Course is the most difficult to play, yet others would single out the New as worse, partly due to its length, the inward half being a 'long slog'. The Old Course is undeniably full of natural subtelties, of appropriate penalties for poor shots, and this is why the greatest golfers, Bobby Jones and Jack Nicklaus among them, have in the end come to love it.

74

Professionals and amateurs tee-up on the Old Course in front of the grimy stone mansion housing the Royal and Ancient Golf Club (the 'R & A'); and, every golfer knows that, from the 'big room' windows, their stance is being monitored by the members.

The oldest golf club, for which we have written evidence, is the Gentlemen Golfers (now the Honourable Company of Edinburgh Golfers) which was formed in 1744. Nevertheless the Royal and Ancient club is the most famous in the world. On 14th May, 1754, some 22 Fife 'noblemen and gentlemen' had formed themselves into 'The Society of St Andrews Golfers' to play annually for a Silver Club over the Links at St Andrews, the winner to be 'Captain of the Golf'.

During January, 1834, King William IV agreed to be patron of the Club which thereafter was styled 'The Royal and Ancient Golf Club of St Andrews'. In those days the 'Union Parlour', then on the site of the old Grand Hotel (now the students' residence of Hamilton Hall), was used as a Clubhouse. The present Clubhouse was opened in 1854.

Commonly just called 'the R & A', with its membership of some 1750 (the club with the highest membership in the United Kingdom is the Wentworth, Virginia Water, Surrey, with 1850 members), the club is still private and is the Governing Authority for the Game of Golf through the greater part of the world. Consequently the Club is constantly being called upon to give advice where golf is developing and expanding. In the showcases of the R & A are many old clubs dating from about 1760, and a wide selection of early golf balls.

Membership of the R & A is by 'invitation' and prospective members are throughly vetted; those whose only wish is to have 'He was a member of the R & A' placed in their obituaries are rigorously weeded out. To wait around for membership is to linger for dead-men's shoes, and members have to attend some 35-40 years to get a locker in the 'big room'. The club does allow Supernumary Members, who must be over 70 years of age and have been a member for 20 years; these members pay a reduced fee, but cannot play. The machinations of Women's Lib cut no ice at the R & A, who still bar women from cluttering up the consecrated carpets.

Incidentally, apart from the R & A, the town has four golf clubs; The St Andrews Golf Club, the New Golf Club, the St Rule's Ladies Club, and the St Regulus Ladies Club. All these clubs have their premises in Links Road, which runs down the left hand side of the Old Course.

Rule-making continues to thrive at the R & A, but the famous caddying trade has declined since the introduction of the caddie-carts in 1949, when the 2nd Baron Brabazon of Tara (d.1974) first wheeled such a contrivance on to the Old Course (a practice now banned). As one sports correspondent once said: 'The golfer who doesn't take a caddie at St Andrews denies himself the wine of the country.'—and the caddies remain a colourful bunch, walking in the footsteps of the inimitable Donald 'Blue' Mitchell and 'Poot' Chisholm. The caddies were all known for their ascerbic wit, as a former Bishop of London found out. His Lordship blasted his ball from the infamous Hell Bunker and said, 'Out of Hell in one!' 'Aye, m'laird,' grunted his caddie, 'and ye better tak that club with ye when ye dee.' One high-scoring player was once told by his caddy: 'It's an acoontant ye need, no a caddie.' When another golfer ended up in yet another bunker he complained to the caddie that he had been in too many Old Course bunkers. His caddie agreed with, 'an' there's still twa or three o' them ye haena been in yet.'

Somehow of all St Andrews institutions golf remains unchanging. The problems of 70 years ago are still with us. Then the links were congested, a problem which the opening of the Eden course helped, but today the congestion has returned with a vengeance. Again in 1912 the Old Course was a mess. A 'Report by the Green Committee to the General Meeting of the [R & A] Club on 24th September, 1912' began thus: 'At the Spring Meeting the Green Committee had, unfortunately, to report that "the abnormal drought of the Spring and Summer of 1911, coupled with the enormous traffic, wore out the Links to such an extent that most of the approaches were like bunkers and many of the putting-greens had no grass left on them."' Water pipes were suggested and in 1914 the Town Council agreed to supply water for all the four St Andrews courses. This water, and the modern use of weedkillers and fertilisers has inhibited the performance of golf balls. Who today—because of the texture of the grass—could rival the longest recorded drive of the American Craig Ralph Wood (1901-68)? Wood, in the Open Championship of 1933, at the fifth hole, drove his ball an estimated 460 yards over the parched ground. Today, the 'St Andrews shot' (a long running shot) is still favoured. The R & A, with their 'Implements and Ball Committee' are forever trying to prevent the golfball manufacturers from ruining the game by providing balls which make the courses too short—with all the bunkers in the wrong places!

'Forgan is one of the best known names in the club-making trade, and wherever golf has penetrated, clubs turned out by this firm are to found.' So one correspondent to the magazine *Golf Illustrated* reported about Messrs R.Forgan & Son in the early 1900s. Robert Forgan (1824-1900), who learned club-making from his uncle Hugh Philp (1782-1856), took over the latter's business in 1856, and by 1890 was employing fifty workmen. In 1863-64, when the Prince of Wales was elected Captain of the R & A, Robert Forgan made him a set of clubs which won him the ultimate *imprimatur* to legend all his wares 'By appointment to His Majesty King Edward VII'; the Prince of Wales's feathers were impressed below the maker's name.

The firm's golfballs, the *Forgan* and the *Acleva,* for years, were favourites with golfers worldwide; and the firm boasted (in the 22nd September, 1899 edition of *Golf Illustrated*) that they alone employed a man to hand-hammer golfballs to give them extra drive and straightness. Forgan's premises were situated on the modern site of the 'St Andrews Woollen Mill'. Such well known names as Auchterlonie and Anderson (who set up their own businesses) learned their trade from Forgan. Robert Forgan, too, pioneered the use of the hickory shafts, and he bought his wood (from Quebec) at the Dundee Docks. Museums and private collectors and golf clubs today still prize their Forgan clubs. In St Andrews the modern trade of golfclubmaking is carried on by such as J.B.Halley & Co. Ltd. and the Swilken Golf Co. Ltd.

For more than 200 years, of course, the only accepted golf ball was a 'featherie', a sphere packed with down. Then in 1845, a St Andrean called Robert Paterson produced a ball of *gutta-percha* (a substance obtained chiefly from the latex of Malaysian trees of the Sapotaceae genus), only bettered by the rubber-cored ball of 1899, still used today.

Without the combustion engine St Andrews would be as isolated in terms of transport as it was in the 18th century. The railway first arrived in St Andrews in 1852, and the line was run from 'the corner of the field near the golfer's first hole, Links of St Andrews', some four and a half miles to the Edinburgh, Perth and Dundee Railway at Milton, near Leuchars.

The prime movers in having a railway were Provost Playfair and Robert Haig of the distillery family. Thomas Bouch—to win infamy through his work on the Tay Bridge—was the engineer. The line opened on the 1st July, 1852 and was worked by the E, P & D line. By 1858 the railway line was found to be badly in need of renovation—a consequence of Bouch's shoddy workmanship—and was not strong enough to take the increased traffic and heavier engines, so extensive repairs were undertaken. The railway helped to bring tourists to St Andrews on excursions but the locals complained that 'many of the excursionists often [*were*] in a state of intoxication'. The station of the day was on the site of the Old Course Golf and Country Club, while the stationmaster's house became the 'Jigger' inn. In the early days a trip to Leuchars took 20 minutes at 13.5 m.p.h. The East Fife Railway linked St Andrews to the East Neuk lines on 1st May, 1887, and a new station was built in a gully by City Park. The East Fife line was closed to passengers in September, 1965 and the line was abandoned in 1966. On the 6th January, 1969 the branch line from St Andrews to Leuchars was closed.

Before the construction of the Forth Bridge (1883-90) a journey to St Andrews from Edinburgh was tedious. A train was taken to Granton, then there was a short walk to the ferry followed by a 30 minute steamer crossing and a walk to the station at Burntisland with probably a change of trains at Thornton Junction; thereafter a journey to Leuchars and another change for the train to St Andrews.

A telegraph office was opened in St Andrews in 1870 and the first telephone was obtained by Robert Niven, Flesher, in 1885. The university had the first established mail system in the town during the eighteenth century linking with the university at Edinburgh. The town, it seems, had a postal service of some kind by 1755, but the roads were too hazardous for mail coaches. Yet by 1813 the burgh was the terminus of a mail gig from Perth/Edinburgh; and the town's first postmaster, George Mitchell, died in 1833. In 1858 St Andrews only had one postman, William Mackie. One Provost, George Murray, was postmaster in 1863 and operated from Union Street. In those days there were no post-boxes in the burgh and letters had to be 'handed-in' to the postmaster.

The town's first postmaster in the modern sense was George Cruickshanks, who carried on a postal business from a shop in South Street. The office then moved to Union Street, and from there to a room in the burgh surveyor's office in the Town Hall. The last site before the present post office was opened in 1907, was within the Christian Institute (from 1892), Church Street, from where it had moved from the 'Citizen Office'. Ellice Place post office was opened in 1898.

Printing began in St Andrews around 1552. St Andrews received its first local newspaper, the *St Andrews Gazette,* in 1862. The paper was published by Melville Fletcher from his South Street premises and ran until 1883. The present newspaper, the *St Andrews Citizen,* dates from 1870 and has been published continuously. The site of the present 'Citizen Office' occupies the land on which was located the

73. The north elevation of Links Road overlooking the '1st and 18th' of the Old Course. St Andrews Woollen Mill is on the site of the golf club factory of R. Forgan & Son, established by Robert Forgan (1824-1900). Down this row are the town and ladies' golf clubs, while Rusack's Marine Hotel dates from 1887.

74. A *feu-de-joie* is fired outside the R & A to celebrate the crowning of Edward VII, 9th August 1902. The soldiers are probably the 'Heavy Battery' of the St Andrews branch of the 1st Fifeshire Royal Garrison Artillery Volunteers.

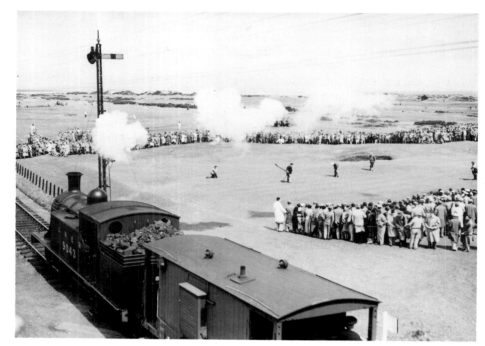

75. In the days of the railway the trains from St Andrews station have excellent, if fleeting, views of some of the finer golf shots.

premises of Baillie Bell (the father of the Rev. Dr. Bell of Madras College fame) who practiced his skills as a type-caster. Alexander Wilson—'the Father of Scottish Letter-Founders'—Bell's erstwhile collaborator, was responsible for the first casting of the Dollar sign for use in America.

From the mid-18th century sea-bathing had been publicised in Scottish newspapers as an efficacious treatment for a wide variety of complaints. So folk had come to St Andrews to bathe to cure 'ulcers, scabs, scaled hands, itching, leprosy, corns, tumours, pains in the limbs, hydrophobia, all inflammations, all catarrhal effects, nephritis, gonorrhoea and arthritis', from the early 1800s.

Initially men bathed naked in the waters around St Andrews. As Victoria's reign developed, the burgh council fell in line with others, ruling that a swimming costume must be worn. By the 1890s costumes were universal and the fashionable female St Andrews bather wore a lace and braid-trimmed blue-serge costume, with shoes, stockings and cap. The rule was to be all-enveloped so that lust should not disturb the delicate Presbyterian conscience. The sexes were separated for sea-bathing and bathing-machines were a regular feature on the West Sands (they remained until the early 1930s). These machines dated back to the 1860s in St Andrews, and were really sheds on huge iron wheels. Bathers changed in them and when the machines were pushed into the water by the more Amazonian fish-wives earning pin-money, the bathers descended from them into the icy water. Having no swimming-pool of its own the St Andrews councillors segregated 'official' bathing-places; they organised a 'bathing station' on the West Sands run for many years by a town worthy called Maggie Stark. The women bathed at the castle beach and men by the Step Rock. From the early 1900s a precarious changing hut on stilts was sited at the Step Rock until the, now boarded up, concrete bathing-houses of the 1930s were erected.

Introduced to the seaside in the latter part of the 18th century, donkeys were utilised first by women in rides along the beach. They were once the preserve of the horse-coupers. Today the beach entertainments have disappeared from the East Bents with only the evangelical missionaries supplying music and mummery with a religious theme for the tourist. The children's play area on the East Bents of modern times is a far cry from the Pierrotts who were intoduced from France by Clifford Essex in 1891. A popular group of Pierrotts in St Andrews were Burnaby, Newcombe and Proby's 'Bachelor Boys'.

Up to World War II the southern end of the West Sands was used for fire drill by the City Fire Brigade, for parades by the local militia volunteers, and Sunday promenading. And the sands were used for motorcycle racing from 1908 to the early 1950s. Today the cycles have been replaced by the sand yachters. These days the bandstand at the Bow Butts lies silent, but once the Scores rang to the brass

78

bands. A popular ensemble was that of the boys of the Training Ship *Mars,* once moored in the Tay for the 're-education' of the area's young scallywags, rendering the typical seaside music:. 'I do like to stroll along the prom, prom, prom, where the brass bands play, tiddly-om-pom-pom', from the popular song *'I do like to be beside the seaside.'*

Linking the town's maritime interests with the university and present day exploration, the Gatty Marine Laboratory is situated on the East Bents, that strip of land between the upper harbour and the sea. Primarily a research institute of the university, the Gatty offers courses in Marine Biology in a laboratory first established here in 1896 and named after Dr C.H.Gatty who endowed it when the former wooden building, a temporary fever-hospital, burned down. Indeed, the university had the first marine laboratory in Britain dating from the 1880s.

At the East Bents too, is the old lifeboat shed—where the long-defunct St Andrews lifeboat *The John and Mary Hadfield* was established in 1910—now the headquarters of the sailing club. St Andrews had its first lifeboat in 1801, one of the first to be built in Scotland. This was changed again in 1823 and 1859, whereupon the celebrated *Polly and Lucy* was purchased. This vessel served until 1873 when the *Ladies Own* was bought and saved lives until 1892, to be replaced by the *Lucy* until 1910. Here at the East Bents was where the salmon fishermen dried their nets and dumped their gear. In 1926 a putting green was set out and the footbridge over the harbour was opened by the popular Provost William Lamond (d.1928).

Coastal erosion has always been a problem in St Andrews. For a hundred years succeeding town councils have conducted a make-do-and-mend policy. One year it would be the castle buttresses which cried out for attention, another time the West Sands, but government money was never available, and the then County Council did not see it as a problem. The regular planting of *ammophilia arenaria,* known as marram grass, along the West Sands has helped fight the erosion of sea and wind. Along the walkway by the sea outside the cathedral walls, the last resting places of the medieval dead are oft times disturbed by cliff erosion. The exisiting wall was begun hereabouts during 1856-57. Today the Regional Council has agreed to sponsor the preservation scheme for the area between the harbour and the castle at a cost of £176,000. And, a further scheme for the cliffs area west of the castle is needed too. Indeed, since medieval times, a considerable erosion has taken place, and some 3ft is lost in certain places every storm. Still to be seen by the adventurous is St Rule's Cave, also known in the past as Lady Buchan's Cave, as the said denzien is noted as having fitted it out as a grotto in which she held tea-parties. One man who concerned himself with reclaiming land from the sea was burgh councillor, George Bruce (1825-1905), whose eponymous embankment leads the modern road round to the West Sands. This embankment sculpted the old town rubbish dump, with the help of sunken barques, into the modern foreshore.

The idea of a theatre in the Old Byre of the Abbey Street Dairy Farm was first conceived by Alexander Brown Paterson, M.B.E.. (b.1907). A journalist by profession, Alex Paterson was the theatre's Administrator until 1980, when he retired after over fifty years as a playwright, actor and theatrical majordomo. The theatre was founded in 1933 and the guiding lights of the enterprise were members of the St Andrews Play Club which had begun in embryo among members of the Hope Park Church Bible Class.

Plays were performed in very spartan surroundings from 1933-36, then 'theatre regulations' had to be compiled with, and after refurbishing a new performing licence was granted in 1937. Thereafter each summer the Play Club presented a repertoire of plays for both visitors and residents. Activities were called to a temporary halt when war broke out in 1939, but the Dundee Repertory Company were able to stage performances from time to time while their theatre was being reconstructed. The first St Andrews Repertory Company was formed in 1940 and somehow the theatre managed to keep open until the end of the war in 1945.

In 1969 there was the final season in 'the Old Byre' and preparations were made for a new theatre opened by the celebrated Scottish actor, Andrew Cruickshank, in 1970. Today the theatre flourishes and is the setting for both professional and amateur shows. For its size St Andrews does well to be able to support a live theatre (the Crawford Centre also stages plays) and a cinema.

Despite its former importance in Scotland's ecclesiastical and political affairs, St Andrews has figured little in the royal history of Scotland since James VI of Scots became James I of England in 1603 and disappeared to London. In 1982 H.M. Queen Elizabeth II made one of royalty's rare visits to the town. Charles II received the keys of the city in 1650 at the West Port while on his progress to be crowned on New Year's Day at Scone, 1651. Those keys were not to be delivered to royalty again until H.R.H. Edward, Prince of Wales, received the Freedom of the City in 1922. This was the occasion too, when Earl Haig and his A.D.C. General Arthur Blair set up the royal visit in which the Prince of Wales

76. 'Auld Daw' Anderson served drinks and lemons to thirsty golfers on the links; Peter Anderson (n[e]
relation) enjoys the ginger beer. Rumour has it that 'Auld Daw' had 'speerits' for the golfers he favoured

received an honorary degree from the university. Edward 'played himself in' as Captain of the R & A in 1933, following in the footsteps of his brother H.R.H. George, Duke of York, who became Captain of the R & A in 1930. On 27th September, 1876 H.R.H. Prince Leopold, Duke of Albany (Queen Victoria's fourth son and eighth child, known as the 'Scholar Prince') had become Captain of the R & A and stayed at Mount Melville with the Whyte-Melville family. A third royal duke, H.R.H. Prince George, Duke of Kent, became Captain of the R & A in 1938, but had visited the town in 1937 to receive an honorary degree from the university.

Incidentally it was Prince George of Kent who was the second recipient of the name of St Andrews in a title. In October, 1934 his father, King George V, created him Earl of St Andrews, on the occasion of his marriage to Princess Marina of Greece. The prince's grandson, George Philip Nicholas, born in 1962, holds the title today. H.R.H. Prince William Henry (later King William IV), the third son of George III, was created Duke of Clarence and St Andrews in 1789. The title merged with the Crown in 1830.

H.M. Queen Elizabeth the Queen Mother has made a number of visits to St Andrews. In 1927, as the Duchess of York, she visited St Leonards School for the school's Jubilee, and again in 1962 and 1977. On 20th September, 1950 she visited St Andrews to celebrate the 500th anniversay of St Salvator's College. In 1929 she officially opened the Younger Graduation Hall. During 1942 a foreign king, Peter of Yugoslavia, visited the town with the Polish Prime Minister in Exile to review the Polish Troops serving as a part of Fife's Coastal Defences.

Only three commoners have had St Andrews in their enoblement. The first was the Liberal Chancellor of the Duchy of Lancaster (1846), John Campbell (1779-1861), who was created Baron Campbell of St Andrews. In 1892 the distinguished scientist and Liberal M.P. for the Universities of Edinburgh and St Andrews, Lyon Playfair (1818-98) was created Baron Playfair of St Andrews. His son, George James Playfair (1849-1939) became the second baron of that name, and the title became extinct on his death.

Since medieval times, St Andrews has always welcomed 'strangers within her gates'. Some have just visited to pray, others to learn, and still more have elected to spend the rest of their lives here. Owing to the fame of Andrew Melville (1545-1622), a St Andrews *alumnus* and founder of Scottish Presbyterianism, who became principal of St Mary's College in 1580, students came from Denmark, Belgium, France and Poland, for instance, 'whilk crabbit the king muckle', said a contemporary chronicler, for Melville was no royal favourite. Interestingly enough, almost four hundred years later the town was to welcome more Poles, but under different circumstances.

77. A diligent cameraman zooms in on a youthful Arnold Palmer on the 18th green.

78. Doug Sanders and Jack Nicklaus with the Open Championship Trophy over which they fought a memorable battle at St Andrews in 1970. The Open Championship was inaugurated in 1860 at Prestwick, Ayrshire; the first Open to be played at St Andrews was in 1873. Jack Nicklaus won the Championship again at St Andrews in 1978. The Open Championship is run wherever it occurs by the Royal and Ancient Golf Club of St Andrews. When held in the town in 1984 it specially marked the 150th anniversary of the event in 1834 when King William IV agreed to become royal patron of the Club.

79. John G. Salvesen, on the morning of 2nd September 1983, 'plays himself in' as Captain of the R & A. Rick Mackenzie, the caddie who retrieved the golfball, is rewarded with the traditional sovereign; this custom goes back to 1806. Laurie Auchterlonie, Hon. Professional of the R & A, completes the group.

80. H.M. Queen Elizabeth the Queen Mother with Miss Martha Hamilton, Headmistress of St Leonards at the school's Centenary Celebrations 1977.

81. Former Prime Minister Harold MacMillan talks to actor Andrew Cruickshank on the occasion in which they both received honourary degrees from the university, July 1977.

82. A.B. Paterson takes a last look at the Old Byre Theatre before its demolition in 1969. This picture, taken by Tod, shows the old workshop on the right and the theatre on the left.

83. The power and intensity of the 'Diary of Anne Frank' at the Byre Theatre 1982, as portrayed by Rose McBain, Joyce Deans and Malindi O'Rorke in the production by Adrian Reynolds. The play was given a national tour in the Byre's Jubilee Year of 1983.

84. Tears form on the railings of the gateway to the cathedral at the east end of North Street.

85. Low tide at the East Sands with St Andrews rising in a soft haze; on this site the town began its long history.

The Polish soldiers arrived in 1940 and caused a stir with their distinctive uniforms and cloaks, and the enthusiastic way they sang on the way to morning service at the Roman Catholic church on The Scores. The soldiers were billeted in the hotels, church halls and private houses in the town, and carried out duties as a part of the coastal defence garrison. Some of them continued their university education here. The Polish staff officers had their headquarters at Cupar, and the Commander-in-Chief of the Polish Army in Scotland, General Wladyslaw Sikorski, had his main base at Forfar. Today a colourful mosaic panel on the wall of the Town Hall speaks of the gratitude of Polish soldiers who had received hospitality in the town during World War II.

Over the years St Andrews has developed some important and interesting links with the United States of America. On 17th August, 1976, a Bicentennial Banquet was held at University Hall to mark the fact that the American Declaration of Independence (1776) was signed by three *alumni* of St Andrews. Benjamin Franklin (1706-90), the American statesman, scientist, inventor, printer and author, visited St Andrews in 1759 and was given the degree of Doctor of Laws by the university, while the town made him an Honorary Burgess. James Wilson (1742-98) had been born at Carskerdo, near St Andrews, and was a student of the United College of St Salvator and St Leonard when he was fifteen years of age. He left Scotland in 1765 and became Professor of English Literature at the College of Philadelphia. The Rev. John Witherspoon (1723-94) was created a Doctor of Divinity at St Andrews in 1764 'in recognition of his signal abilities and leadership', and was a delegate to the Continental Congress.

Americans have always been at the top of the list when it came to major university endowments in the modern years of the university developments. Andrew Carnegie is perhaps the best known, but the American multi-millionaire and philanthropist, Edward Stephen Harkness (1874-1940), is worthy of mention. In 1930 he established the Pilgrim Trust and through his donations residential halls for men were financed as well as the restoration of the University Chapel.

Undoubtedly the earliest links between St Andrews and the United States were formed through 'St Andrews Societies'; one opened at Charleston, South Carolina in 1729, to be followed by Philadelphia, Pennsylvania in 1747, Savannah, Georgia, in 1750 and New York State in 1786. A similar club was founded in Halifax, Nova Scotia in 1768.

Change is constant, change is inevitable; the city and royal burgh of St Andrews has been changed—stripped of its former honours if you like—into a seaside appendage of the N.E. Fife District to the greater glory of party political collectivism. But St Andrews will never die, cannot die, for the town is loved, and there will always be enough people who care to make the town survive.

86. St Andrews Bandstand (1905) and the Martyrs' Monument (1842) at the old archery practice ground of Bow Butts.

87. From the tower of the College and the Collegiate Church of St Salvator this circular picture takes in almost the whole of modern St Andrews, from the medieval town centre to the municipal and private housing schemes to the south.